OEDIPUS
VARIATIONS

Studies in Literature and Psychoanalysis

Spring Publications, Inc.
Woodstock, Connecticut

Dunquin Series 19

"Oedipus: Two Essays" by Karl Kerényi English translation
© 1990 by Spring Publications Inc. All rights reserved
Originally published in German in Karl Kerényi's *Oedypus, Volume I*
(first published 1966) and *Oedypus, Volume II* (first published 1968)
and subsequently in his *Collected Works, Volume IV* (*Gestalten und
Entwürfe*), © by Albert Langen Georg Müller Verlag
Herbig Verlagsbuchhandlung GmbH, Munich, Germany
"Oedipus Revisited" © 1987 by James Hillman
All rights reserved

Published in 1995 by Spring Publications, Inc.
299 East Quassett Road, Woodstock, CT 06281
Text printed on acid free paper
Printed in the United Stated of America
Cover design by Julia Hillman and Brian O'Kelley

Library of Congress Cataloging-in-Publication Data

Oedipus variations: studies in literature and psychoanalysis
p. cm. — (Dunquin series ; 19)
Includes bibliographical references.
Contents : Oedipus / by Karl Kerényi ; translated from the German
by Jon Solomon — Oedipus revisited / by James Hillman.
ISBN 0-88214-219-4 (pbk.:alk. paper)
1. Oedipus complex. 2. Oedipus (Greek mythology) 3. Sophocles
— Characters — Oedipus. 4. Oedipus (Greek mythology) in literature.
5. Psychoanalysis and literature. 6. Freud, Sigmund, 1856-1939.
I. Kerényi, Karl, 1897-1973. Selections. English. 1991.
II. Hillman, James. Oedipus revisited. 1991.
BF175.5.O33O38 1991
150.19'5 — dc20   90-21611
CIP

Contents

OEDIPUS: TWO ESSAYS

Karl Kerényi

1

OEDIPUS REVISITED

James Hillman

87

Acknowledgments

Jon Solomon gratefully acknowledges the careful reading and editing of his translation by Magda Kerényi.

Passages originally in French in Karl Kerényi's essays were also translated by Jon Solomon.

James Hillman's "Oedipus Revisited" is based on a lecture given at the Eranos Conference in Ascona (Switzerland) in 1987, and its original publication appeared in *Crossroads*, ed. Rudolf Ritsema, Eranos Yearbook 56—1987 (Frankfurt a/M: Insel Verlag, 1989), pp. 261–307.

Oedipus: Two Essays

KARL KERÉNYI

I.

The *Oedipus* is essentially a tragic analysis. Everything is already there, so it needs only to be extricated. This can be seen in the simplest action and in the briefest segment of time, even if the events themselves are still very intricate and dependent on particulars. How favorable that is for the poet! But I fear the *Oedipus* is one of a kind without any secondary species. . . .

Schiller to Goethe, 2 October 1797

1.

The *Antigone*, Sophocles' greatest humanistic achievement, never had in posterity the influence allotted in our century, albeit in another way, to another stimulating tragedy by the poet—the *Oedipus Rex*. This stimulus could perhaps have emanated from a more modest work—for it is with the production of the *Antigone* that Sophocles first becomes established as a tragedian—if its contents involved destiny of the same sort. For this tragedy concerns not the immediate, overpowering effect of that which for a poet in particular is artistically and humanistically successful, an effect on countless, joyous audiences, people who had awakened themselves to the spiritual stimulus toward a new self-understanding. Instead, we find at the outset the effects on a single man, one who has induced this stimulus.

This stimulus, or movement, is called "psychoanalysis." It emanated to a certain extent from the *Oedipus Rex* of Sophocles, and then Sigmund Freud reapplied this tragedy or rediscovered the seed. A dividing line between reapplication and discovery would be difficult to draw. The familiarity of Oedipus in the world of today and one exalted idea in the series of archetypes of humanity depend on it and the great impression which Sophocles' tragedy made on Freud. Therein he discovered the archetype of the analytical method, whether or not he knew the aforementioned words sent by Schiller to Goethe. But before we examine the literary tradition, we must discuss how the portrait of Oedipus, without known or unknown psychological meaning, emerges as the basis of the variegated and abundant ancient legacy.[1]

2.

As king of Thebes, Laius, the great-great-grandson of Cadmus and then also kin to Dionysos, grandson of Cadmus, had chosen for his wife a great-great-granddaughter of Echion, the 'Snake-Man,' an original Theban from the 'dragon-sowing.' She was the true, indigenous Theban, since Cadmus had immigrated there from Phoenicia. The name of Laius's father was Labdacus, his wife Epicasta or Jocasta. With the latter name she achieves a fame scarcely achieved by any other queens, mothers, or wives of the Greek heroes, but she had to combine these roles vis-à-vis one and the same hero. It is through her that even her brother Creon acquired temporary mastery over Thebes. There is a legendary version in which Laius had killed his father-in-law. So throughout the whole mythical tradition it seems as if Jocasta was the source of royal power in Thebes, for in this city royal power corresponds to matrilinear relationships.

Laius, however, should not have generated a son by her. Three times the Delphic oracle had warned him: only if he died childless would Thebes remain safe. Laius was not able to maintain his firm resolve—so Aeschylus described the progenitor of Oedipus—but it happened, almost an insanity, that the newlyweds carried out their marriage. It would have been possible for Jocasta to fulfill only her matrilinear function, but she was no mother, at least of Laius. Otherwise the story of the oracle could also be explained through the words of Jocasta at the beginning of the Euripidean tragedy *The Phoenician Women*.

Laius had already lived long years in his childless marriage to Jocasta when he determined to ask the oracle about his progeny. The Delphic god answered him, "Sow no offspring against the will of the gods! You will produce a son who will slay you and annihilate in blood your entire house." He should have set his mind at ease and desired no issue. But overcome by passion and wine, he engendered a son with Jocasta and then exposed it after birth. After more long years he set out, driven by evil forebodings, to learn from the oracle whether the exposed child was still alive. He took the shortest route from Boeotia, through the region of Phocis, toward Delphi and reached the narrow crossroads where he was to be murdered.

The third and simplest report from the oracle fashioned the antecedents to Sophocles' *Oedipus Rex*. Laius and Jocasta were warned at Delphi that their son would kill his father, and so they exposed the child. The older mythographers turn their attention more to the figure of Oedipus found in still older myths and less to these antecedents. His name ac-

tually means "Swellfoot." One applies sufficiently
this peculiar and, in a crude and archaic mythologem, very intelligible name in the Homeric spirit
to account for and make credible that he in fact
makes reference to the feet of the exposed youth!
It is obvious to think of an extremely phallic being,
indeed, one of the Dactyls born from the earth, sons
of the great mother of the gods, or simply a son born
to the soil, darling of Mother Earth. In the post-
Homeric *Theogony* written by the Boeotian poet
Hesiod, not once did she shy away from incest!

In the mythology of this hero the feet of the youth
are indeed caused to swell. He was exposed in a jar
in the winter (this is the version in Aeschylus's *Laius*
tragedy). And to increase his helplessness this also
was said to have been done to him: his feet were
pierced with a golden brooch or "a sharp spike." So
his entire life he had this "swellfoot" and was called
by that name thereafter. From his ancient Dactylic
nature perhaps, he remembered that he was red-
haired and easily burst into fits of rage. We also have
an inclination to associate him with pedigreed
stories of exposed heroes and divine offspring which
identify him as a solar progeny, almost a son of the
Sun God Helios. He, like Perseus, was exposed in
a chest to the water, either the Euripos, the flowing
sea which divides Boeotia from Euboea, or the Corinthian Gulf.

In this way he reached the vicinity of the city in

which Polybus, a son of Hermes, ruled, whether this be Anthedon, Corinth, or even Sicyon. Queen Periboea, whose name refers, just as does that of Polybus, to many herds of cattle, was laundering her clothes on the shore as the chest landed — a heroic tableau. In a so-called "Homeric goblet," one sees that it is Hermes who presents the child to the queen and that she places it in the lap of the king. Oedipus brought no bad luck to this couple. He grew up in the house of Polybus with the belief that it was the house of his parents. It was only according to the well-known version that he was exposed not in the sea but on Mt. Cithaeron where the shepherds from Thebes on the one slope and from Corinth or Sicyon on the other customarily gathered together.

In these historical antecedents to *Oedipus Rex*, the Theban shepherd hands the child over to a Corinthian, who brings it up as his own and then presents it as a gift to his childless king. In this tragedy Oedipus himself explains how at a banquet he, who had become the noblest citizen of Corinth, had a drunken guest throw in his face that he was not the son of his father. This situation was the creation of Sophocles; it reflects not the heroic age but life in contemporary Athens. Whereupon Oedipus secretly set forth to Delphi to question Apollo. But Apollo did not answer his question. Instead, he threatened him with the horrible fate that he would marry his mother and be the murderer of his father. Therefore

Oedipus dared not return from there to Corinth but took another direction, through Phocis, and reached the crossroads where he was to become a murderer.

It is not important for us to know exactly where these narrow crossroads lie. Father and son were to meet there without recognizing one another—an unfortunate father and an even less fortunate son who should have mutually avoided each other and also did everything to ward off their encounter. This, their *knowledge* about their fate, was not in any way, however, necessary. The choice of this crossroads in particular and of no other between Thebes and Delphi, viewed from this sort of practical view, must *also* be considered as the fate. The crossroads themselves were the fate. Schiller believed "the oracle had a share in the tragedy, which is not to be replaced by anything else at all." But in the realm of a completely realistic human story of such an encounter between father and son, knowledge of their fate was not necessary; the story is also conceivable without the interference of the oracle.

Narrators to whom the oracle is important assume something here that from the beginning establishes the essence of their narration on the *unintended* and consequent murder. Oedipus did not suspect in any setting of the tale that his path would run into that of his father. Therefore the murder was by itself not a case for Freudian psychology!

It more likely could have been Laius's apprehen-

11

sion about being dethroned. There was absolutely no need at all of an oracle as instigator, for the archetype was already there in divine history in the story of Uranos and Cronus, an extremely ancient tradition from both Greece and Asia Minor. In this story Uranos, the husband of the Earth, was also her son—and in that no less a holy tale. The exposition could have existed from that apprehension alone without the instructions of Apollo, but it could not have been without his knowledge if he was already the oracular god of Delphi. This is not obvious as the transmitted presentation of this story, for which oracular opinion corroborates the human experience: how often one races into the horrible out of fear for the horrible!

So this very human event came to pass: the encounter in a narrow pass where avoidance was completely impossible. Laius was leading in his vehicle, and his herald cried out to the unknown traveler who was coming from the other direction, "Traveler, make way for the king!" The anger boiled in Oedipus. He said nothing but strode silently forward on his way. One of the king's horses stepped on his foot. The elderly gentleman now struck him on the head with his staff, as it is told in the *Oedipus Rex*, and the measure was full. The son "angered and unknowingly," as one reads in an ancient mythological handbook,[2] took his staff and struck dead his father and then the herald. For his portrait of the hot-tempered

Oedipus Aeschylus added this detail as well, that he bit into the body of the dead man and spat out his blood.

It was an older form of the story in which Oedipus at that time was bent on horse theft and Laius accompanied by his wife Epicasta. According to this version, after the murder Oedipus fled into the mountains, as is still the custom today in Greece, and did not touch Epicasta, his unrecognized mother. But how could she then, in the later development of the story, which always remains the same, have voluntarily taken the murderer as her husband even though she was witness to the murder? Everything seems proper in that older version in which he shows the same outburst of his quick temper: the son struck the father and seized the mother whom he took unknowingly to be his wife. The queen is to this extent added to his booty, and through her comes mastery over Thebes—a circumstance possible in a matrilinear society.

From this version of the story we can clarify that gap found in the later settings, for in the *Oedipus Rex* one must take notice and be surprised that Oedipus makes inquiries only after many years as to how and where his predecessor died. In all the variants the incest could have been discovered earlier or later. In matrilinear systems incest, something deeply desired, was under the mightiest of taboos. It was forbidden except to the divine primordial-mother but so much the more to mortal mothers. The sons were, as can be observed in primitive societies, even sent over to other families so that they would not commingle further with motherly blood. In the patrilinear society of the heroic epoch, this conviction was not so strong, or at least not so uniform. This becomes apparent within the context of an epic setting—one of the literary predecessors of Sophocles—which we must still briefly examine before we proceed to the *Oedipus Rex*. In the *Phoenician Women* (382) of Euripides, Jocasta speaks of her situation more as one of misfortune than as an infamy. This interpretation seems also to correspond better with popular Athenian sentiment and to those of Sophocles who made his own the strongest condemnation, although Jocasta did not consider her incestuous dreams to be something serious.[3]

In every version Oedipus is victorious over the sphinx, the destructive demon-woman because of whom there is a mountain called by the Thebans 'Phikion.' While he is not, however, always the solver of the riddle, he does display courage and strength. This better suits his original, earliest characterization according to which he spent his days in the mountainous regions around Thebes. This variant, of which there is only a hint in the *Oedipus Rex* (1143), that the shepherds brought him up on Cithaeron, is completely feasible. Sophocles chose the version with the riddle. After Laius's death Creon, the brother of Jocasta, assumed power; the story can to this extent be reconstructed, wherein the role of the queen's brother as de facto dictator is a matrilinear trait. Here lies the deepest basis for the Sophoclean Oedipus's mistrust of Creon. Otherwise, the story offers us traits corresponding to the known historical circumstances. The Thebans met in council daily in the marketplace and considered the riddle which the sphinx had posed to them. From her mountain, or having flown onto a column in the middle of the city, she sang her riddle: "There is a two-footed creature on the earth, and a four-footed one called by the same name, and also a three-footed one. It alone of all living creatures that dwell on the earth, in the air, and in the sea changes its form. It strides upon the most feet supporting itself, and then the speed of its limbs is the least." So long as the sense of these words was not understood, the sphinx daily snatched up one of the Theban youths. Then came Oedipus.

"Man is what you mean," he exclaimed, "since after he is born he crawls around on the earth and is four-footed, but when he becomes old, he bears a crooked neck under the load of old age and uses his staff for the third foot and is three-footed." Whoever discovered this solution spoke the essence of Apollo, on whose temple in Delphi already in Sophocles' era had been carved "Know thyself"—a riddle whose solution was "That you are a man." If the poet in the *Oedipus Rex* had wished only to proclaim wisdom from the religion of Delphic Apollo, the essentials would have been no farther from our grasp than what he declared clearly at the very outset. And so he would have had a man suffer and be destroyed in a manner concealed by the Apollonian way! Such a man turns out to be Oedipus the riddle-solver, and as a reward he takes, besides the control of Thebes, his mother to wife, and with her he was to issue four unlucky children: Eteocles and Polynices, Antigone and Ismene. Is not one horrified at this prize, especially when one knows that incest for Sophocles is an unthinkable abomination?

3.

Homer knew of a conclusion to the Oedipus story in which only the mother, because of her true, queenly sense of shame, sacrifices herself. Odysseus saw her in the Underworld:[4]

> Epicasta, the beautiful mother of Oedipus,
> Who unknowingly committed an act
>   stirring astonishment,
> Married her beloved son who had
>   murdered his father.
> But soon the gods brought it to light.
> From this time on in beloved Thebes
>   Oedipus ruled in misery
> Through the gods' ruinous decree over
>   Cadmus's stock.
> But she descended through the gates of
>   mighty Hades.
> Tied in open despair to the high rafter
> With a strangling rope, she left unending
>   misery
> behind, the result of the mother's vengeful
>   spirit.

Homer, who knew this as well, could emphasize the difficulty that Oedipus had later in life, even if he had not blinded himself, wherein he fell in battle with a mighty crash and din and won the appropriate honors through funeral games in Thebes.[5]

An epic poem from the Theban cycle to which Homer alludes, the *Oedipodeia*, contains this further information about Oedipus's life to which one or even two new marriages belong. Two names at least are handed down as wives of Oedipus after Epicasta or Jocasta. He would have had children with them first since the doubled relation to his mother in this story was discovered quickly. "One unbroken constitution of archaic magnitude"[6] can be said of this Oedipus. He was nevertheless unbroken even in the other epic, the *Thebais*. As an old man, blinded by his own hand and inclined to outbursts of fury more than ever, Oedipus cursed his two sons who reciprocally killed each other. Jocasta lived after this version, in the condition described to us by Euripides in the *Phoenician Women*.

From this very human and moving subject matter emanated an evocation to the tragic stage, at first in a tetralogy by Aeschylus in which the extant *Seven Against Thebes* was preceded by two lost tragedies, the *Laius* and the *Oedipus*, followed by the satyr play *Sphinx*. So it was not Sophocles who first filled a shadow with life and meaning and elevated it to an unforgettable form, as in the case of Antigone, a small and marginal character in Theban epic. The distinction and circumspection with which the Sophoclean Oedipus makes his appearance, the majesty of an extraordinary mortal, to whom after his death would be allotted the cult of a blessed hero, could have been characteristic of him already in Aeschylus. But this characteristic of Oedipus, attested by his hero's grave in Boeotia at Eteonos and the locus of his disappearance in Attica at Colonos Hippios, Sophocles apparently portrayed not in that early period of his life in which he wrote the *Oedipus Rex* but later, at the end of his career, when he produced the *Oedipus at Colonus*. It is the majesty of a *tyrannos* of Periclean type which stands in the forefront. That was the style of the time, one must say, and therefore it is Sophoclean! Still, majesty and style are important also in connection with the means through which Sophocles elevates this tragedy, as he does the *Antigone*, which is on the level of prophecy.

The circumstances have been clearly articulated and (in the words of a philosopher, "Where everything lies open, there is not to clarify") lie open for the spectator but not for those entangled in destiny. Their situation would have been known since childhood to the Athenian theatergoers. Why the epidemic? Why this loathsome, bleak state of multitudinous death with which the Athenians were familiar—from their actual experience in the recent past? And then one hears, if not the very first, at least the first significant words from the kingly Oedipus:[7]

19

Pitiable children, it is well known
to me why you have come! For I know that
Sick as you all are, no one among you
Is sick as I.

It is the famous "tragic irony" wherein the speaker
speaks an ambiguous speech without knowing it.
The poet, who has put these words in his mouth,
and the public understand it is over his head! In this
case, however, insofar as the events unfold, they
understand as well essentially what Sophocles in-
timates, that is, that the royal personage who believes
that everything is settled in his life suffers from a
confusion which he does not know he bears. He sees
only the epidemic which rages outside, while the
necessary cure is often right there where there appears to be health! Jocasta has already said it with
the same words at the end of her "Analysis of Life,"
urged on by Oedipus with his self-destructive rage:
"I am sick enough!"[8]

From the ancient Theban story, which has been
confirmed by philological study,[9] came the tragedy
of vision, a universally valid 'Ecce Homo.' The chorus
sings,[10]

Who bears, who bears
More luck than
So much

As the vision
And after the vision his downfall?

Apollo destroys the vision. Then cries Oedipus, after he has blinded himself:[11]

Apollo, it was Apollo, friends,
Who brought me this injury, my injury!

Everything proceeds according to that last bit of wisdom from the Apollonian religion, as Pindar proclaimed:[12]

What is someone? And what is no one?
Man is the shadow's dream!

But did Sophocles proclaim this with razor-sharp accuracy and not something more precisely human? Must we not place great importance on that word expressed from beginning to end—"sick"? Would not the physician be able to come closer to what is real in Sophocles than would the philologist? Freud did not make it easy for himself in his explanation since he perceived the effect of the play only in Oedipus's murder of his father, while Oedipus, to be sure, insofar as the motive of the perpetrator is concerned, was no father-killer! That the hero sinned without his knowledge and against his intention he understood[13] "as the right expression of the *unconscious* nature of his perpetrated endeavor," a general, human necessity, of which fate and the oracle were the materialization and which, as we must add, Oedipus carried within himself as a hidden, agitating sickness. Sophocles meant only Oedipus's general confusion, so he touched as well on that human suffering which Freud believed to be perpetually connected with the search.

The kind of human existence Sophocles described in his Oedipus was as it appeared to him more and more in his own life. Already earlier in the *Antigone* he described it as demanding help, even in death, and now he describes it as needing a cure, until death.[14] In 442 B.C., the end of a peaceful era in Athens, the *Antigone* was produced, after which his fellow citizens and spectators chose him as one of the commanders-in-chief who were to restore the democracy on Samos. It is said expressly that there was a wish to send the poet of the *Antigone* there along with Pericles. In 430 B.C. began the worst crisis under Pericles—the epidemic. The Athenians also believed that Apollo sent the sickness as he had promised in an oracular response to the Spartans.[15] In the following years, according to all indications, the *Oedipus Rex* was created. That the Athenians understood their poet literally when he spoke of the sickness is easily demonstrated. When several years later (420 B.C.) they sent to Epidaurus for the cult of Asclepius, the healing son of Apollo, they broke the journey of the god, replaced by his substitute serpent, at first in the house of Sophocles. He had himself dedicated an altar to him and composed a poem for the cult. He served as Priest of Amynos, a sickness-prevention hero in Athens, and after his death he earned himself a heroic cult under the name 'Dexion.' This name alludes to the fact that he had welcomed and greeted properly with the right hand the god of healing.

4.

The transfiguration of Oedipus after his death from the one who murdered his father and married his mother to a beneficent hero—a historical fact worth consideration since his hero's grave and the account of him are consistent with one another—began in his homeland, Boeotia, on Cithaeron. There is an account about it as well. If he was originally to be buried in Thebes, the Thebans did not at any rate tolerate it. He had been characterized by his bad luck, and the thought did not enter their minds that he could also bring good luck as a result. So the burial was moved to another town in Boeotia. Mishaps occurred in that town, however, and the inhabitants believed that they were caused by the grave. Therefore, they finally buried Oedipus secretly by night at Eteonos on Cithaeron. They knew not that the place happened to be in the sacred precinct of Demeter, the great Mother-Goddess and Earth-Goddess. It was the homecoming, and it was granted by the Delphic oracle. The place is even called "the Shrine of Oedipus."

There was, however, thanks to the poets and mythographers, a greater *mythos* than the only one in his homeland. In the deme of Colonos, on the threshold of Athens, they told the account of how

in his voluntary, painful travels at the end of his life
the blind Oedipus reached that "knoll" that was and
is "Colonos," and there, on a place dedicated to Demeter Erinys, he went beyond to the Underworld.
This deme was Sophocles' birthplace.

According to ancient opinion the poet presented
his deme with his tragedy *Oedipus at Colonus*—one
"of the wondrous!"—and made it famous.[16] He was
over ninety. He foresaw his own transcendence and
adapted his seeing eyes to those of the blind Oedipus in this way: an Athenian poet attached to a future holy hero precisely this oddity, that his last encounter was to be at his very birthplace. None of his
tragedies are as visionary as this one. It is not astonishing even among his translators that a poet, con-
sidering his own death, chose the *Oedipus at Colonus*
for translation, as it were, Sophocles' funereal escort.[17]

Sophocles had Aeschylus as a dramatic predecessor for this play. His *Oedipus* could not have been
written with the same kind of experience and knowledge as the last play of Sophocles. It must, however,
be assumed that even Aeschylus's play concerned the
other world and felt strangely familiar to the people who had been initiated into it at Eleusis. The
poet was accused of disclosing the Mysteries. He
must have been acquitted, though, because he
proved that he had not been initiated in Eleusis. It
was a celebrated case of "Lack of Intention"[18] because one could indeed identify a similarity between

the vision of initiation and an appearance on the stage in Aeschylus's *Oedipus*. The similarity between the poet's representing the encounter with the great mother goddess of the Underworld and the Eleusinian religion made a correspondence thoroughly possible, although Aeschylus probably did not want to imbue the public with the proper vision of the initiation and kept himself at a distance from the Mysteries of Eleusis which established pride in *his* native community.

Of the Aeschylean *Oedipus* only so much can be deduced with certain probability: its most essential event was the death of Oedipus,[19] whose location was at Eteonos. There stood his hero's shrine, which perhaps already in Aeschylus's era had the inscription[20] in which the grave and even Mother Earth speak: "On my back I bear mallow and asphodel from a thousand roots; on my bosom the son of Laius, Oedipus." Eteonos lies outside Thebes and yet within its vicinity; that is to where the blind hero ought to have been relegated by Creon and his own sons.[21] It seems that Oedipus cursed his sons in the first half of the tragedy, just as in the *Thebais*. And at Eteonos, at the end of the tragedy, the goddess appears to him. She was ready to take him to her bosom and to release him finally from the curse of his deed—from the Erinyes of his mother. That or something similar, a work of the poet from Eleusis, served as a model for the poet from Colonos.

It might have been because of this that Sophocles similarly connected his *Oedipus at Colonus* with the Mysteries of Eleusis but without disclosing them.[22] Greater circumspection prevailed for Sophocles as did greater consciousness of what constituted high art, more so probably than in Aeschylus's case. His play moved in that direction, although its visibility is, to be sure, further in the background, and thus he could have been accused on account of this. The unspeakable, that which one cannot divulge, lurks behind the scenes in Sophocles. In the forefront arises the sacred hill, and through this rocky nucleus bronze stairs lead to the Underworld. The poet indeed knew every tree. It is all dramatic "historical painting": the arrival of the old, blind man with Antigone—the Antigone made famous by Sophocles—her initial admission onto Attic soil, the admission itself being effected by Theseus, the Founder-Hero of the Athenian state, the refusal of Creon, the curse to Polynices, to the point where Oedipus undertook to lead the metaphysical background of Greek tragedy into the Land of the Dead.

These pessimistic verses had already resounded:

> Not born to be surpasses
> all! But one is already there,
> again to go, from where he came,
> hurrying. That is the second blessing.

This song no longer sounds completely negative when it can refer to the entrance to the benevolent gods of the Underworld, to the underground Dionysos, and to the motherly mistress of the Land of the Dead, those who send the living creatures up and then take them back again to themselves. To them the tragic heroes return. Oedipus does just this, a great example for all, at first before the eyes of the onlookers, then in the narration by the messenger. The blind man has already *seen* Hermes, Leader of the Souls, and Persephone, the mistress of the Dead, when he cries out:[23]

> This is the direction! Only follow me.
>   Leading me
> Are Hermes the Companion and the
>   Queen of the deep!

The messenger reports also of an audible cry which comes from the divine side: "Listen, Oedipus! Why are we still waiting? You tarry too long!"[24]

If the scene with the apparition of Hamlet's father were to be lost, nothing significant for our knowledge of Shakespeare, the hypotheses of his dramatic poetry, or of Elizabethan drama in general would be missing as a result! Not the same can be said with regard to the essence of Greek tragedy and its hypotheses if the world were deprived of the *Oedipus at Colonus.*

5.

Freud did not believe that the effect of the *King Oedipus* could be just that of an unparalleled work of art. The spectator reacts, according to him, "to the hidden sense and content of the saga. He reacts[25] as if through self-analysis he had recognized the Oedipus complex in himself." The tragedy, we must understand, is

> fundamentally an immoral piece. It abolishes the ethical responsibility of men and shows divine powers which direct offenses and the impotence of man's ethical emotions which defend themselves against the offenses. One could easily believe that the saga material aims towards an accusation of the gods; in the hands of Euripides, critical and at variance with the gods, there probably would have been such an accusation.

Freud's belief in the incomparable thematic impact of incest as the subject of a tragedy and its anticipation vis-à-vis Euripides was already refuted by this poet himself.

The survival of the *Phoenician Women* among the extant tragedies of Euripides escaped Freud. It means that the tragic interpretation of the incest is moderated not only in looking back at the Sophoclean *King Oedipus* but also at the *Oedipus* by Euripides himself. This tragedy has been lost, and the restoration of its contents has not been successful in all phases of the plot. Euripides clearly tried to have a greater impact than Sophocles, so he apportioned the discovery of the identity of the murderer of Oedipus's father and the husband of his mother into two phases and introduced two royal women onto the stage. The second was Periboia, the foster-mother who came from Corinth to announce the death of her husband to Oedipus; this was to comfort him so that he would not any longer need to fear fulfilling the oracular warning that he would kill his father and marry his mother. Perhaps she cherished the hope that after discovering the secret of her foster-motherhood Oedipus would return home as husband and king.

When she arrived, however, Oedipus already understood that he was the murderer of Laius, but he did not yet understand that he was also Laius's son. Creon had assumed power, and Oedipus had been blinded by Laius's old comrade-in-arms. Periboia probably would have taken him home even in this condition, so much the more in fact since he had certainly been exiled as well. Now as it turned out regarding Jocasta, the unknown identity of mother and loving woman brought forth an ideal portrait of the wife, a highpoint in the celebrated Euripidean cognizance of women. Jocasta does not yet know that the blind Oedipus is not just her husband, and she wants with complete submissiveness to follow him in exile. There is a duet on the ideal marriage,[26] which both (Jocasta in trochees) offer in a singing voice. Periboia is overcome with this mutual song of praise, a triumphant song of marriage, and in the next instant comes the second discovery with an impact that must have surpassed that of the progressive, step-by-step discoveries in the Sophoclean *Oedipus*. We do not know from where it came or what effect it had. Oedipus was already blind, and it is not believable that Jocasta could survive, according to the laws of tragic climax, past the most tragic point of the drama. The discovery of the *incest* does not constitute the highpoint of the tragedy, however, as much as does the *discovery for itself* which shattered the only possible luck of an unlucky human couple.

It was possible for the tragic poet to grasp something even more hideous in an incest-tragedy. Although our knowledge of ancient dramatic poetry is limited, Seneca did just that in the crassest form. For the prototype for his *Oedipus* the Roman did not choose Euripidean tragedy, although these had long since been read and performed. The illustration of one exemplar which was current in Italy is preserved for us in a plastic reproduction on an Etruscan cinerary urn.[27]

The Sophoclean *King Oedipus* was nonetheless classical, and Seneca intended to make a Latin reproduction. Characteristic for the Roman poet and for his Italic culture, which also produced Etruscan funerary urns decorated with tragic scenes, is its distinction from the Attic work. Instead of tragic analysis we have a death-oath, the violent overture to the Underworld. Laius is conjured up from the Land of the Dead. While the gloomy ceremony proceeds behind the scenes, the chorus summons Bacchus—i.e., Dionysos—in the foreground. It means the same for Oedipus as it does for a Roman emperor: he is not allowed to come into contact with such a celebration.[28] Instead of the spiritual shock on *truth's* way, which Oedipus trods before the Athenian spectators, we discover the details of an Etruscan-Roman *prophecy* from the entrails of slaughtered victims. Laius's knowledgeable spirit unveils the whole secret. Oedipus does not need to search for it, only to defend himself against imaginary enemies. It is the great opportunity for the Stoic philosopher Seneca to let his chorus sing about Stoic fate and to show one which even surpasses the oracle, since on account of Oedipus the mother also had to kill herself. In his form of destiny, the incest was the only part of the whole which the spectator recalls to mind under the weight of the terror found in *fatis agimur*—"Destiny compels us."

6.

When Rousseau received a report that the young
Voltaire at eighteen was writing an Oedipus for the
stage and had already read it aloud to different
groups, he wrote to his informers:[29] "I have a very
good opinion about the young man; nevertheless
I am dying of anxiety as to whether he did not di-
minish the terrible in this great theme [*grand sujet*]
because he was confusing it with love [*y mêlant de
l'amour*]." Voltaire did so and was on account of that
censured by good art critics and Sophoclean schol-
ars. But, after the play by Corneille, he could not
help but do it and had therefore difficulties with
the actors as well, for they did not find sufficient
"*de l'amour*"—one must say it in French—in the
piece. They let him wait four whole years for a performance. They did not anticipate a "thrill" from
the incest and its discovery!

From the highest degree of "repression"—this is
the way Freud from his standpoint must comprehend the reaction of the French in the seventeenth
and eighteenth centuries—Corneille in giving an
account of his *Oedipus* shows why he could not easily use the masterpiece of Sophocles or Seneca—
characteristically these were two exemplars which
he could not distinguish any further—on the French

stage.[30] I hope he did not fear that that part of the saga on which, so Freud believes, the impact of the piece rests would offend the delicacies of the women (*"la délicatesse de nos dames"*). Singly and alone Oedipus's bloody self-blinding scene gave him concern, as did the absence of love from the whole tragedy. He helped by introducing a loving Theseus and a Dirce who grants him her love in return. He invented her to be the daughter of Laius and Jocasta and also a neglected pretender to Oedipus's throne.

The greatest distance from Sophocles' triumph must be established here unrelated to the Freudian point of view. No one would wish to trace the ruin in the same theme, that of Sophocles, back to the "repression." The first step toward the dissolution consists of the loss of the spiritual tension in Seneca, the substitution for which is an apparition which the French accepted unhesitatingly, albeit moderated to dream-appearances. The second step Corneille achieved by eliminating the concentration on one, single, internally and externally endangered person—Oedipus. When he takes Jocasta as well with himself, *his* ruin from the beginning is supposed to threaten and not be mingled with that of the smaller prince, for which Voltaire found the politically inflammatory words *"Rien que le fils d'un roi!"*[31] With greater consciousness Voltaire completely reconcentrated the tragedy. This was possible for the theater of his era during which the expansion of political elements, something inherent in the mistrust of the Sophoclean Oedipus, was much more appropriate.

This expansion began with Corneille and his reflections on the relationship between the two kings, Oedipus and Theseus. In Voltaire's *Oedipus* the spectators thought to identify references to well-known contemporary sovereigns both living and dead, even if these references were not intentional. Voltaire made Oedipus relevant in this way and not from the incest motif. He placed what Freud had expected from Euripides, a pioneer of new thought, more properly the area of the psychoanalyst, in the mouth of Jocasta who was destroyed in the wake of Oedipus's destiny:[32] "*J'ai fait rougir les dieux qui m'ont forceé au crime.*"

7.

A further step toward the dissolution was conceived of by Platen. He gave an Aristophanic twist to the process of decomposition and created within the tradition of this play a literary satire and comedy in a veritable satyr-play, *The Romantic Oedipus*. What is peculiar about this satire is that it belongs quintessentially to that tradition. It provides the most objective justification of the Sophoclean *King Oedipus* in its classic incomparability to the intellectual detour of a *deductio ad absurdum*—the consequential continuation of that path which Corneille, after Seneca, followed to well-known absurdity. The tragicomedy begins with the French "Love" between Diagoras and Zelinda, called by Platen Periboia, Oedipus's foster mother; she takes on, as expected, a romantic name. This pair's mutual relationship leads those between Theseus and Dirce, and Philoctetes and Jocasta, representing romantic elements which have no part in the classical drama, into a greater amount of comedy. We wonder at Platen's critical spirit on the objective plane: what does not escape his notice is that which merits mockery by a superior intelligence schooled in the classics, and at the same time he sees through the inner loci of its denoument.

We should not discontinue our wonder here, however, where *The Romantic Oedipus* operates in the subjective sphere. The parabasis of the Attic comedy, in which the poet is allowed to have the chorus speak directly for himself, permitted Platen to speak unexpectedly about the "Lüneburg Heath," a symbol for Germany, whose sheep, the little sheep, provided for a genuine Aristophanic animal chorus. For months during the years 1827–28 he worked in Sorrento, Capri, and the Pontine island of Palmaria on this acknowledgment of the "true tragedy." Insofar as it is not, in order to create it, and—as it is called at the commencement of the parabasis—

> To show whence it starts depends not on
>   the comic poet's opinion,
> To whom it is enough if he teaches from
>   what Siren's song he needs to flee.
> And from this his creative faculties now
>   prepare a living example for you.
> Surely he lives far away. . . .

We hear where he lives at the conclusion of the last choral passage:

> To Pinienhain on the inlet of the sea,
> Where the wave drains completely the
>   dripping foam,
> He goes wilfully alone, and provided that

37

no ear
Eavesdrops on him further beyond the
   mountains,
Then no approval of the befriended goads
   him on to song
But an abundance of his own harmony.

There appeared a real disciple of Sophocles as a student of Aristophanes—an extraordinary spirit, that serves as reminder. This reminder will draw attention to what "the public" of the time doubted and what is said as a simple word about this theme in the right place:

The tragic art suffers . . .
. . . purely the pure human nature of the
   passion.

II.

The world depends on its mothers.

Hofmannsthal

1.

The second and last work which appeared in book-form from the poet of the *Hyperion* before he went completely insane was *The Tragedies of Sophocles Translated from the Greek*—Hölderlin's version of the *Oedipus Tyrannus* and the *Antigone*. If we keep this designation as a "version" in mind, we will most effectively do justice to our undertaking. Hölderlin had in mind not simply what his publisher, Friedrich Wilmans in Frankfurt am Main, advertised when the book appeared in 1804,

> A classic translation, an achievement in its art. . . . The philologist who compares it with the original will find it observes throughout faithfulness, precision, and the spirit of the German language. The educated reader, even without knowledge of the original language, will

41

sense in reading this work the purest pleasure
of heart and spirit.[33]

If the reader is seeking in Hölderlin's work the
realization of this generally valid ideal for a translation, he then has to establish the breakdown which
necessarily had to obtain in the face of contemporary criticism.

The philologist who today sees at least a "curious,
precious creation" in these "translations from Sophocles by Hölderlin" and keeps some distance from
such a style but would also at the same time be ready
and willing must yet find that the

> misunderstood words, confusions, and uncom-
> prehended references are so interwoven
> throughout the translation of both dramas that
> on average every fourth or fifth verse is con-
> fused one way or another. That means that
> Hölderlin's German wording penetrates only
> gropingly and in an exceedingly conditioned
> way into the Greek wording of Sophocles, while
> in Sophocles he develops himself sharply and
> precisely in speeches of his persona and of the
> chorus. The general as well as the special state
> of destiny under which Hölderlin had trans-
> lated the Sophocles was impeded extensively
> and in many individual ways since one finds
> in addition to what we learn in Hölderlin what

Sophocles (and his characters) had said naturally and decidedly from his certain world.[34]

In 1905 Wilhelm Dilthey spoke with great intensity and respect for human reality in his truly classic
essay about Hölderlin as translator of Sophocles, as
if of a sick man.

> His rhythmic sense is not impaired, his speech
> resounds, and he extracts its deeply moving
> sound of pain. But he has lost his mastery of
> the Greek and confused known words with
> ones sounding similar. In his notes lie before
> us, like a heap of rubble, the poetry of his bet-
> ter days. It is irritating, and in penetrating fur-
> ther one becomes wearied and disappointed
> and refrains from yielding to its senseless, hid-
> den reverie. Its incapacity to retain any logical
> connection is manifest.[35]

The sense of the notes lies, it is more correct to say,
not in the logical-theoretical plane but in their practical and spiritual self-preservation.

Ambivalent, seriously perplexed. Those were the
feelings of Karl Reinhardt whom Hölderlin's verbal
"blunder" had long since repelled. Then Carl Orff's
music redeemed the *Antigone*—this happened again
later with the *Oedipus Tyrannus*—so after the pre-
miere in 1951 a word about "Hölderlin and Soph-

ocles" was awaited from this great philologist. He succeeded at best in putting into words for us that particular type of deviation from the general ideal of a translation's truth which Hölderlin wished to achieve, representing which we now possess his version of the two tragedies; if they are somewhat of a failure, at least they exist on such a higher, self-selected plane of failure than that of a poor translation.

> Tragic for him is a type of revelation or prophecy stripped of the self. . . . Sophoclean tragedy is for him a piece for redemption and newly aroused divine fulfillment. . . . The possibility of further arousal is assured through the rhythm of the age of spirit. The dramas of Sophocles are rediscovered holy texts—rediscovered because of preparation for one new divine visitation. As he understood everything at the time, he experienced as well his ancestors, his shock, his damnation, his veneration, his suffering, and everything which might appear to us as objective as a moment of "rapacious time." Time is for him the ecstatic in which Being reveals itself.[36]

For all that, in Hölderlin's *Notes to Oedipus* we also find his unpretentious hypothesis about god, who "is nothing but time." Yet he could not have the distance and the overview of the whole he created at that time as did the philologist for whom the parlance of Heidegger's existence-philosophy, according to his explanation of Hölderlin, is of assistance in expressing his interpretation. The poet spoke of his duty as translator, which he saw singly before him, much less distinctly. By thinking about it he was already almost carried away to a higher plane from which he was free to use these words (to the publisher):

> I hope to improve the Greek art, which is foreign to us, through national suitability and the errors with which it has always been content; I present it more dynamically than usual to the public so as to stress more the Oriental (which it has disavowed) and correct its artistic mistakes where they occur.[37]

Surely he wanted to know something definitive of what, as he said, was understood—of the "Oriental," i.e., the primitive. We must therefore assume this includes the "Archaic," which Hölderlin also strove for unintentionally with his Greek mythology. The tone, however, is already (28 September 1803) set too high and is characteristic for the latest and penultimate mental state of the poet. It is difficult to establish a threshold between an enraptured state, from which there is a return to the basis of reality, and an insane state of mind, from which this is not possible any longer so long as the not-being-able-to-return proves not to be final. Already in the Utopian vision of the hymn "Celebration of Peace," the boundaries regarding political reality were falling. This itself began to be absorbed in the unreal, special world of the ecstatic Hölderlin. A medial world between history and pure imagination developed in the fancy of first the poet and soon then the translator who adapted his *Tragedies of Sophocles* for this special world. His *Oedipus Tyrannus* came to pass at such a level, his *Antigone* in a still further advanced state of enrapture.

Hölderlin's political path was that of an inspired Republican who was swept along by Bonaparte during the French Revolution. When he heard the first news of the peace of Lunéville (1801), he leapt beyond in the world of pure imagination and, in the first setting of his hymn, greeted divine Peace which emanates from the heavens. Indeed seen from there, where he believed he had firm (political) ground under his feet, from the perspective of his Homburger friend, Sinclair, and yes, even of the princely women of the court, there appeared as well an earthly approximation, thanks to the first Consul, the originator of the peace of 1801, which proved to be possible for the poet's vision. And so the last, genuine written version of the hymn was in appearance earthly. But only in appearance! The mixture of the poetic imagination with historical reality is a mark of insanity. We know not to whom Hölderlin finally entrusted his "Celebration of Peace" as a pamphlet. He thought as well of the publisher who edited his translation,[38] and he dedicated the *Tragedies* to the princess who shared her enthusiasm for Bonaparte in 1799—at this time, however, in a tone which at that moment would not have been possible for him.

Perhaps the Princess Auguste of Homburg was not such an enthusiastic partisan of Napoleon as was her mother, the countess. And yet these lines could be found in her birthday poem the same year in which the General became Dictator:

> Alone, o Princess! Lies
> The heart of the free-born no
> longer in its own blessedness? Then worthily
> Associated with the laurel of the Hero himself,
> The beautifully ripened outlawed. . . .[39]

It is not even certain whether Hölderlin himself had to deliver the ode to the princess or whether Sinclair must have played the intermediary role. Auguste, who had a great but secret love for Hölderlin, answered the "flattering song" with her own intimate lines which are extant. They end in thoroughly ancient praise:

> Your course is so beautifully and surely begun
> that you require not encouragement; only my
> true joy will always accompany your conquests
> and progress. Auguste.[40]

Their relationship did not amount to a dialogue, let alone to an open one. In the "Testament" of the princess—in her later confessions—it is referred to in this way: "I spoke to him in those two years three or four times, strictly speaking *not at all* [her emphasis] and saw him perhaps six times.—But the imagination had free play."[41] She even came close to insanity, but no one was permitted to posit a guess about it, least of all the poet.

In the condition in which he found himself when he sent *The Tragedies of Sophocles* to the printer, he wrote the dedication "To the Princess Auguste of Homburg." The contemporary critic found this quite discourteous and indecorous, even though no one knew that Hölderlin openly answered with a much more intimate ticket!

> You encouraged me years before by a good
> epistle, and I have remained all the while in
> debted to those words. Now, since the poet

amongst us must do something else out of either necessity or kindness, I have chosen this trade, for it is connected surely to exotic but solid and historic precepts. Otherwise, when there is time, I will sing of the parents of our princes and their seat and the angel of the sacred fatherland. Hölderlin

This dedication reflects the contemporary world of Hölderlin; the princess and the poet stand on the same plane, and the poet sees clearly his duty as he approaches life. It is not only the fact that he is a bard similar to those of the Greeks, bearer and harbinger of fundamental, divinely bestowed and propagated song, but because he "amongst us"—in Hölderlin's fatherland—does in addition something indispensable or pleasant. He chose the business of translating. It was a *parergon*, a secondary labor which he performed as well and not with his own tragic poetry like the *Death of Empedocles*! But one ought to ask about the necessity, about the deficiency which was corrected in this way. "Modern poetry is lacking," we read in his *Notes to Oedipus*, "especially instruction and workmanship. That is, the learning process is premeditated, and once it is learned it can then in practice always be reliably repeated." Poetry was a *mêchanê*, an instrument, for the ancients, and tragedy was an instrument of equilibrium. "There is greater equilibrium in tragedy than pure succession." Surely the might of nature exists in anger, and of men the most intrinsic part is "boundless unity," a Colossus which happens "as God and Man form a pair." The representation of the tragic is chiefly dependent upon this, so the poet calculates and reaches the equilibrium either (as in the *Antigone*) leading more from the beginning toward the end or (as in the *Oedipus*) where there is the opposite balance.

Unrelated to this point of view, which the spectator (or the reader) of the tragedy may or may not adopt for his or her own, the pathological, the requisite salvation, is expressed here as nowhere else. The poet sustains precisely this tenor, the "clandestine sense and the contents of the saga," which was so important to Freud,[42] as if a mask. He translated the passages in which Sophocles speaks of the illness of Oedipus and Jocasta pedantically and verbatim,[43] while Hofmannsthal rewrites at the beginning of the tragedy,

> I know the name
> Of all your sorrows, you see; I go to
> Bed with them and arise with them.

And later, from the mouth of Jocasta, "My agony is sufficient."

To the Hölderlin who himself was ill, the illness of Oedipus with its "going to bed" seemed apparently chilling; at least he remained resolved and determined in spite of it. Orff's musical configuration ought therefore to be in the manner of oratorio and with more recitative in the *Oedipus,* but then it should be more like a dirge in the *Antigone.* Hölderlin's concern is therefore generally valid in both tragedies, for they accurately reflect the titular phrases *tyrannos* and *anax.* Among the modern translations and interpretations of Sophocles, Karl Reinhardt decided for the sake of accuracy on at least the Latinate *Oedipus Tyrannus.*[44] For Hölderlin the Greek *Oidipos Tyrannos* had the significance in those revolutionary times of *"Oedipus the Tyrant,"* to whom Teiresias acts as a foil during the "caesura" of the tragedy. The soothsayer in Hölderlin's presentation brings out the relationship of poet to singer. When he needs to translate *tyrannos* and *tyrannis,* he uses "Lord" and "Lordship," intolerable for the "Freeborn" in the ode to the Princess Auguste.

Hölderlin renders *anax* as "king"—"prince" in the *Antigone*[45]—terms which the ancient Greeks allowed in reconciling means of addressing the gods and aristocratic humans. In "Celebration of Peace" he used "Prince of the Feast" to describe Consul Bonaparte in a contemporary, and not at all special, German sense. It is an idle question whether Hölderlin's illness, which had been disclosed as early as 1800, was affected at all by the fact that in 1804 the Consul became the Kaiser. Surely this did not produce the definitive breakdown. The poet did not demonstrate that he was vassal as well to Elector Frederick II of Württemberg when Sinclair was handed over to him on the charge of high treason.[46] The draft of the hymn "To the Prince" reveals this: "What can one think about the Prince when. . . ." It was then "with humility" that "Scardanelli," the completely changed Hölderlin, first expressed himself, and in his letters from the time of his complete mental derangement he is dependent upon no one as much as his mother.

2.

It is more difficult for us today to consider the Oedipus theme—the unknowing father-murderer united with the conscious seizure of all that one desires—as simply a non-political subject and not at the same time as a possible political subject as well. But it had to be recognized at one point for its significance as a general, human possibility. This happened because of Sigmund Freud, and this is a historical fact which we can establish chronologically even if we do not choose to generalize freely the conclusions drawn from this knowledge. Above all, we will not consider literary works in this regard, since from literature there is at least as much to learn for psychology as, in contrast, there is from psychology for literature. Works from our own century should and must also be examined from this point of view, and here we might consider Hofmannsthal, André Gide, Jean Cocteau, and T. S. Eliot.

The first notes on this were recorded before the beginning of this century. Freud writes to Wilhelm Fliess on 15 October 1897,

> A singular thought of general value has occurred to me. I have found amorousness in regard to the mother and jealousy towards the

father even in myself, and I consider it now a universal event of early childhood. . . . If that is so, then one understands the thrilling power of King Oedipus. . . . The Greek saga seizes upon a compulsion which everyone recognizes because they perceive his existence in themselves. Each listener was once embryonic and, as a fantasy, was such an Oedipus; but before this dream fulfillment was pulled into reality, each shuddered with the complete sum of suppression which separates his infantile state from his present state.[47]

After five years, in October, 1902, Freud established the "Psychological Wednesday Club" in Vienna. From this time on, then, one must consider the genesis of an atmosphere surrounding this Viennese circle in which his basic idea created stimulating work even without literary intervention.

In 1901 Hofmannsthal was moved by the character of the Sophoclean "Electra." In the written copy of the piece, dating from 1903, that atmosphere was already traceable, even if the quite profound, psychological elucidation of the bitter character of Hofmannsthal's heroine is his own creation without concrete, documented influence from Freud. There begins a period in which the influence of not only Freud but also that of Bachofen in Hofmannsthal can no longer be divorced from the creative act of the poet and from his reaction to this atmosphere. Although Hofmannsthal in the beginning of 1904 was already busy with an Oedipus at Kolonos project, this does not prove that a performance of the *Oedipe Roi* in the Comédie Française in 1900[48] affected him in this way, as Freud assumed that it should and as he himself perceived the effect to be. On the other hand, a *similar* effect of this theme is at precisely this time a greater possibility than before, and this was probably the basis of Hofmannsthal's Oedipus-poetry, a creation parallel to Freud's psychology, the both dependent on the same insights into the possibilities of human nature.

In September of 1904 Hofmannsthal wished to work on *Everyman* in Venice. There he came upon, as he reported,[49] "a French piece 'Oedipus and the Sphinx,' and its substance pleased me so much that I immediately commenced work on the same subject." The piece was Joséphin Péladan's *Oedipe et la sphinx*, but Hofmannsthal borrowed all the details for his drama from the *Oedipus Tyrannus* with such care that one must assume he had the Sophocles tragedy with him. The attentive reader of his *Oedipus and the Sphinx* must therefore ask himself with which topic Hofmannsthal could have completed the second piece of his projected trilogy since he had already anticipated so much of this drama of self-awareness. So the trilogy project is not only there in writing,[50] it is found in the completed piece itself. There is such complete exposition, such complete preparation—preparation also for a tragedy of Creon—that it is therefore already propelled by such moments of great intensity that it paradoxically became an astonishing fragment, albeit in much regard comparable only to the *Andreas* fragment. Neither with the existing *Andreas* fragment nor with the *Oedipus and the Sphinx* was it possible to increase the intensity further or to maintain it for the continuation.

Who is this Oedipus whom our century caught sight of more accurately and more correctly through Hofmannsthal than through Freud? He is the primordial man who lives in all the violence and killing—the killing of not only the father—and in all the insane rage, of which the fragile Hölderlin as well on occasion was part. His traditional angry nature is already there when he appears for the first time at the fatal "three-roads in the land of Phokis," and it is raised to the degree of a demonic possession of anger intensified. He is a somnambulist of anger. The loyal old servant Phoenix portrayed him this way,

> You can not see yourself when anger
> Shakes you, since you become black as death,

Then white as foam. I have already seen you
Make my heart shudder.

What Oedipus himself said, overlooking the enact-
ment of the deed in which he was the angry
murderer,

> The word slew him already?
> The mere word? Lycus utterly alive?

gives us only a single parallel, Hölderlin's introduc-
tion to the "effective, fatal word" in his *Notes to Antigone*. We find it in a more advanced phase of his
illness which was characterized by fits of rage, the
period of the *Oedipus the Tyrant*. Hofmannsthal pro-
ceeded, poetically, as a genuine explorer into the
pith of an angry soul.

The prophetic dream, which the angry man
dreamt more clearly—and in that nonetheless pleas-
ure-driven—foretold the Oedipus-destiny, as only
an oracle could foretell it:

> —at once
> My hands struck down a man;
> and my heart was drunk with a delight in anger.
> I wished to see his face, yet a cloth
> Covered it, and the dream gripped me
> Now tightly and pulled me to a bed.

There I lay with a woman in whose arms
I rest as a god. . . .

The oracle then had this explanation:

The delight in striking
You have satisfied with your father,
With your mother you have satisfied
Your delight in an embrace;
So you have dreamt and so it is to see.

An individualized destiny dream? The one ad-
dicted to anger and the pleasures of love—love
reserved for his mother!—is punished with the
murder of his father and incest. That is, according
to Hofmannsthal, the oracle's point of view. What
sort of punishment is it, though, if the penitent,
while in the arms of his mother, imagines himself
to be a god? It resounds broadly in the mouth of
Oedipus when he describes an *entirely* individualized
dream: "I dreamt/the dream of life—!" Life is "pur-
sued like lashed water" for Oedipus in this dream.
This however would be the "Dream of Life" after
all—according to Freud! But there is still a mean-
ingful distinction. Laius is for Hofmannsthal a
vengeful customer that provoked and deserved his
deathblow. But the mother! "And yet the mothers,"
said Jocasta,

> The mothers attract everything,
> The blood is strong, the world depends on
> mothers.

Oedipus had still not touched upon a wife. Why not? "On account of my mother!" Unconnected with the reference to the father, the mother stands persistently as the source of the pleasure of love, the godliness bestowed. Accurate here would be the Freudian terminology, that which involves the proper goal of the Libido, the greatest desire! For this desire, the forbidden fulfillment, Hofmannsthal had his own unique words. Mother and son, who are targeted by destiny for this desire, can lament and rejoice, as there it is lamented and rejoiced. They are holy, *sacer*, in the primitive, ambivalent meaning of the Latin word, which I introduce: holy and accursed together! An Oedipus is damned by his destiny—and consecrated as King and Redeemer: "chosen" is therefore the correct word. Thomas Mann used it in his *The Chosen One.*

The sphinx does not give its childish riddle to the Chosen One but exclaims,

> Hail to you, Oedipus!
> Hail, to the dreamer of the deep dream.

—and throws herself, according to her destiny, into

the abyss. Antiope, the mother of Laius, the advocate for the ancient religion of women, shrieked:

> Bacchus, we cry out to you;
> We are of your golden blood!
> Come, Jocasta! Disrobe!
> Who covers her body in misery
> When a god comes to marry you?

The enemy, Creon, extends his crimson garment before the feet of the terrible, chosen couple. And the chosen ones speak:

> Oh my king,
> Oh you! We are more than the gods. We,
> We are priests and offerings, our hands,
> All holy, we are completely alone,
> The world.

In other words, "We are of the primordial ground."

The greatest Hubris? Unrestrained arrogance for which punishment must come? That could be, too, if the allusion were not so deep. It proceeds—unconcerned, with whichever consciousness of the poet—in the direction of the primitive violence which follows upon the union of the feminine with the masculine which was produced from it, the union and completion which the incest taboo in human society prevented. It is an allusion from

which, when it is understood, the deepest basis for
the illness which united Oedipus and Jocasta is evident. How insipid the workings of this dialogue at
the end of the tragedy which meanwhile is nothing
but a song of triumph, the promises of a fortunate
life of the ruler! On it the tragedy of the second
piece should still be established, but there was
nothing more to consider about something so darling and exaggerated as this first drama. This Hofmannsthal probably already saw by the time he completed the last act and adapted it in 1905 as an
accessory, a reserve "presented for the new stage"
and conceived as a means for testing the performance, the tragedy of Sophocles with the title *King
Oedipus.*

3.

"Freud. Freudian. . . . For ten years, fifteen years I have been occupied with this without understanding it," wrote André Gide in his diary on 4 February 1922. He came to the conclusion that it would be the best time to publish *Corydon*, his apology for homosexuality. Dizzying, stirring soundings into the psychological depths, where we can find the explanation that the homosexual shuns the female on account of his mother, as did Hofmannsthal's young Oedipus, are not attempted by Gide. What he took from and what he considered meritorious in Freud he stated clearly (19 May 1924):

> I think that I must be the most thankful to him because he accustomed readers to hearing certain subjects discussed without any objections being raised and without any blushing. What he gives us above all is daring; or more precisely, he rescued us from a certain false and painful shame.

Here we find an acknowledgment of the exposed surface area without any attempt at revealing the depths wherein remains the greatest abundance of all to which Hofmannsthal alluded in his *Oedipus and the Sphinx.* Gide, too, sees Oedipus entirely in the traditional way, for instance, when he first mentions the Sophoclean tragedy in his diary in 1910: "Oedipus, who crosses from the fortune of not-knowing into the misfortune of knowing," through the revealing event, *l'événement révélateur,* this—not the hero—produces the drama. He employed this theme for decades. In 1930, the year in which he brought the drama into its final written form, he complained because "of the tardy growth of his Oedipus" (*des lenteurs de végétation de mon Oedipe*). He had in his conception a piece which ironically should have been entitled *Oedipus, or the Triumph of Morality,* said Roger Martin du Gard. "I should have written the piece earlier," he added (7 May 1927).

Still, in 1920 his friend Martin du Gard made notes on his communications, and we are made surprisingly aware of how this *New Oedipus*—for some time in 1927 the piece must have been called *Le Nouvel Oedipe*—was adapted by Gide: "An Oedipus radiates, imperious because of his success, energetic, unaware of any concerns; *un Oedipe 'goetheen.'*"[51] A Goethe–Oedipus—there lies the emphasis.

Such an Oedipus would not be too different from the Sophoclean riddle-solver and the wise sovereign of Thebes, as he *seems* to be. In Sophocles, nonetheless, Being takes the place of appearance. That was the *l'événement révélateur,* which in about 1920 was the vital point for Gide, too, in this tragedy. The great

transformation in Gide's relation to the Oedipus
theme is that he can now say at that turning point:
"And then, without the occurrence of any new
event. . . ." To this Martin du Gard responded, "An
event? He learns that he has killed his father, married his mother, etc. . . . A mere trifle indeed!"

One of Gide's appropriations of the Oedipus-
model took place between 1910 and 1920. It led to
a brief prose drama—too short to fill an entire even-
ing—which was first given by Pitoëff in Antwerp on
the tenth of December 1931. It was, however, quite
disturbing to the author. It was a work of "deep
necessity" ("*profonde exigence*"—31 March 1930), yet
for the entry in his diary—and in this way it became
public—Gide sensed a necessity to plead further
and write this defense for his ("*le mien*") *Oedipus*:

> There is in my facetiousness, triteness, and im-
> propriety almost a constant need to warn the
> public: You have Sophocles' play, and I am not
> in a position to rival him. I leave the pathos
> for him. But look at what he does not under-
> stand and what he left unseen and then at what
> the subject offers in addition and what I under-
> stand. I say this not because I am more intelli-
> gent, but because I am from another era. I in-
> tend to let you see the wrong side of the scene,
> something that ought to shake you emotionally.

> For this is not something that matters to me
> or which I am seeking to attain. It is your in-
> tellect which I am addressing. I have in mind
> not to make you tremble or weep but to ponder
> about yourselves.[52]

Lying herein is certainly a rivalry. It is clearly dependent on time, yet it is dependent as well on Gide's unshaken youthfulness and indomitable immaturity, his everlasting puberty, which Goethe, his ideal, attributed to genius but is characterized by, in addition to great boldness, many transformations. What Gide boldly and consciously strove for his whole life was a Hyperhellenism. He wanted to be a Super-Greek. What he repressed was the ambivalence of the *sacrum* (in which sphere of life—the sexual not being excluded—it is always observed as well) and its ambivalence even among the Greeks. This is the *aidos*, the sense of shame before the gods, the fright before the Mysteries, exactly that which filled the first and largest half of Hofmannsthal's *Oedipus and the Sphinx*. To observe the repression, which is characteristic for Gide, in its full significance, one should harken to this characterization of *The Counterfeiters*, his novel of 1926:

> This novel is somehow untrue in its very basis.
> Marcel Proust also treated the problem of love

between homosexuals. . . . On the whole contemporary society spurns such a passion as well
as whoever yields to it, whose sin is, according
to Proust, what he calls *l'opprobre*, the disgrace,
which he took upon himself and in which he
attempted to feel at home. In his *The Counterfeiters* Gide suppressed precisely this very important side of reality; his men live as if the
whole world tacitly approved of their lifestyle.
He suppressed that their burdensome shame
compromises perception even in their own
eyes; he suppressed the fact that such a man
does not dare to see himself in his own eyes.
He says this because he, Gide, also belonged
to them but did not have the courage to look
at himself and his reality in his own eyes. In
this way Gide had not only created the new-
fashioned observation of the soul but simul-
taneously also established his limits.[53]

The expression of this critic—in the concrete
form: not to be able to look at the whole truth with
his own eyes—is exceedingly to the point. To Martin du Gard's great astonishment, what Gide in
general wished not to see and what he therefore
could accommodate only with difficulty, the not-
wishing-to-see, the erasing of his own eyesight in his
Oedipus-model, was the situation of living in

"shame"—"*l'opprobre*." By this he refers to a sense of shame which society can relatively comprehend, yet when it is a matter of incest, frightful and seductive, the ambivalence transcends the relativity. The most difficult problem is this, to determine with which motivation his Goethe–Oedipus, Gide's Super-Greek, blinds himself if he—just as Gide—was somehow prevented from seeing the horror in incest.

To be consistent and to keep within this Goethe–Gide-nature, this Oedipus should not blind himself. What was already there for him to do? To live in matrimony with his mother and to raise his children? "If my sons are also my brothers, I will not love them any less."[54] He approved even their incestuous wishes regarding their sister, when he was fortuitously the witness to their conversations. He brought unsavory playroom dialogue to the stage. Gide went this far, as he believed, with Freud. But he went only that far and remained there. His Oedipus threw this deception entirely in his own face. Through it, Oedipus in the person of his mother marries his complete *past*, although he was called from his *future*. As a blind man he would proceed contrary to it. The "past" is the word for the mother, who should be expelled at all costs! That Oedipus saw it bare and therefore had to be punished was the initial sense of the blinding. "That which my eyes should not have seen"—these words remain even in

Gide. He struck himself, however, remarkably uniting the old motif with a new sense, even if his drama was already written.

How difficult it was for him on the pre-selected but purely intellectual level to reach beyond the self-evident reality in the tradition is indicated already by his melancholy remark from May, 1927: "I should have written the piece earlier—namely at that time, when he, despite Martin du Gard, was so easily able to slip away with the '*événement révélateur.*'" This was always rather difficult for him; indeed he was older. The blinding was in the narrated piece nothing other than "to enter into this night populated by happy memories which alone are able to restore his optimistic vision of the world, a taste of life."[55] During this period of such melancholy insight Gide took on as a project, in addition to his *Nouvel Oedipe*, a *Dialogue with God*. In it he certainly championed his "heroic humanism" against the conventional religious point of view,[56] although he foresaw only the possibility of an *Oedipus, or the Triumph of Morality* on the stage. For all that, he sketched the agent of the victorious morality, Teiresias, who is Christian in the style of the French past. This also applies to his Creon as courtier, and even in fact to Antigone who in this way of thinking was a nun. Moreover, on 10 May follows this puzzling entry: "No longer *Le Nouvel Oedipe*, but better: *The Conversion of Oedipus.* To me this title seems excellent."

In the drama, however, there is no discussion of any conversion. The blinding is an incalculable act of liberation from the net of god, from the oracle which did not say this exactly, typical within the style of the Gidean *actes gratuits*. "To devise some rash deed to astonish you all, myself, and the gods." So reads the explanation in the drama, but it continued not to satisfy Gide. The drama was not yet presented (18 January 1931), when he was already planning an epilogue in the form of a dialogue between Oedipus and Theseus. Theseus was the other super-hellenic ideal which Gide modeled after the young and the very old Goethe. The plan was realized as an epilogue to *Theseus*, the spiritual testament of Gide, which, completed by May, 1944, appeared in 1946. There we discover what Gide meant by the conversion of Oedipus—an introversion with which he in part reverted to his conception of 1920. The prototype for a dialogue between Oedipus and Theseus is given in Sophocles' *Oedipus at Colonus*. Gide's *Theseus* could to some extent and in certain places be considered his *Oedipus at Colonus*. At least the monologue of Icarus contains this in the form of a question and with some misgiving: "Which great *mother* gave you birth, ye manifold figures?" (The emphasis on the word goes beyond Gide.) And through the mouth of Theseus Gide speaks also candidly about his own, never clarified relationship to the blinding. We must hear both figures to under-

KARL KERÉNYI

stand what Gide realized from the Oedipus-theme
and also what he experienced in himself:[57]

> In this horrid assault against himself was
> something which I could not comprehend. I
> imparted my astonishment to him. But I must
> confess, his clarification did not satisfy me;
> perhaps I did not understand it well.
> —Certainly, he said to me, I have given an
> impulse to the anger; I could set it right only
> in opposition to myself; for whom in particular
> should I have restrained myself? In view of the
> enormity of the indictment and horror which
> had disclosed itself to me, I paid attention to
> the domineering necessity to protest. Besides,
> I wished less to destroy my eyes than the cloth,
> the decoration before which I tortured myself,
> the lie in which I no longer believed, so that
> I could penetrate to reality.
> But no! I did not bring to mind anything cer-
> tain; it was a matter of instinct. I have put out
> my eyes in order to punish them for this—that
> they had not wished to see something which
> lay open in broad daylight and which, as one
> says, must have leapt into my eyes. But in real-
> ity. . . . ach! How should I explain it to you? . . .
> No one understands the cry I then uttered: "Oh
> darkness; you are my light!" And you under-
> stand it just as little as anyone else, which I per-

70

ceive. One heard a lamentation, but it was a confirmation. This cry meant that the darkness brightened itself for me at once with a supernatural light which enlightened the spiritual world. The cry should mean: Darkness, you will be my light from now on. And while the azure firmament covered itself for me with gloom, my inner heaven bestarred itself at the same moment. . . .

In my youth I seemed to be quite clairvoyant, at least in my own eyes. Was I not first to be able to solve the Sphinx's riddle? But ever since my own body's eyes through my own hand took away the world of appearance, I think I have actually begun to see. Yes: while the outer world covered for ever my body's eyes, it opened in me a new line of sight toward the unending perspective of an inner world which I had scorned to that point because only the world of appearance existed for me. And this world which is incomprehensible to our senses is the only true world which I now know. All else is simply an illusion which deludes us and confuses our contemplation of the divine. "One must stop seeing the world to gaze upon god," the blind prophet Teiresias said to me one day; and at that time I did not understand him, as you yourself, Theseus, do not understand me. I am conscious of that.

—I want, I said to him, not to deny the significance of the timeless world which you discovered through your blindness. But what I want to understand but cannot is why you set it against the external world in which we live and manage.

—Since the new perception of truth in these inner eyes made me at once cognizant, I would have been building my human sovereignty upon a crime; everything else would be polluted—not only my personal resolve but even my sons to whom I pass on the crown. So I gave up immediately my claim to an unsteady kingship which my crime had obtained. And you have probably already come to know to which offenses my sons have been carried in my wake and what sort of fate-driven humiliation chains them to what sinful humanity can create. My wretched children are only an illustrious example of that. Naturally my sons as offsprings of incest are especially predestined for that. But I believe that the whole of humanity is disconcerted by one type of primordial fault. Even the best are designated and dedicated to the worst, to the ruin. I also believe that man cannot get along without any sort of divine assistance which purified him from this first contamination and absolved him from his guilt. . . .

You are astonished that I have put out my eyes; and I wondered myself about that. But perhaps still something else compelled me to this rash, terrible deed—some secret need to impel my destiny to the extreme, to intensify my pain, and to fulfill a heroic calling. Perhaps I suspected by chance the lofty and redeeming power of sorrow, but for some reason it had a reluctance also to give in to the hero. Therein it declares itself, I believe, before all his greatness. Never is he courageous until he becomes a sacrifice. He then forces the gratitude of the heavens and disarms the vengeance of the gods. However it might be for the hero, and however lamentable my errors were, the condition of supernatural fortune to which I have arrived compensates me today richly for all the sorrow which I must endure. Without it I certainly would not have reached this point.

—Beloved Oedipus, I said to him, when I realized that he had ceased to speak, I can only praise this type of superhuman knowledge which you acknowledge. But my way of thinking cannot follow yours entirely. I remain a child of this earth and believe that man, no matter who he is and how corrupt he might seem to you, must play out the cards which he has in his hand. Surely it is splendid for you now to turn your misfortune to good and to earn some contact with something which you understand to be divine.

One sees that Gide has not reached beyond the alternative Christian or unreligious, mundane perspective. What the blind eyes of the Sophoclean Oedipus caught sight[58] of remains unseen by him, and unseen as well is the basis for his own human condition!

4.

Cocteau often made Gide nervous, even with his *Antigone*, the Sophoclean tragedy reduced to straightforward, timeless existence which Gide described in a peculiar entry on 16 January 1923 as "ultramodern sauce." Cocteau's persuasion was that he brought the *Antigone* as well as the *Oedipus—Oedipe Roi*, completed since 1925, in book-form since 1928, and *Oedipus Rex*, the libretto to Stravinsky's opera—into the "rhythm of our era."[59] So all the more was Gide allowed to feel stirred to display his type of modernism through the Oedipus-theme, and through his *Oedipe*, on the contrary, Cocteau was stirred to progress to total individuality. *The Infernal Machine*, completed in 1932 and initially performed in 1934, eliminated any reflection with its title. "We obey. The mystery has its mysteries. The gods possess their gods. We have ours; they have theirs. It is that which is called the infinite"—says Anubis in the second act, "The Encounter between Oedipus and the Sphinx." From the sterile atmosphere of a youthful intellectualism we pass over into a spiritual room in which the mother and child reign.

Cocteau's basic premises are "There is the poet and the grown-ups" (*Il y a les poètes et les grandes personnes*). "A certain infantile character is common to all heroic forms of life" (*Un certain caractère enfantin est commun à toutes les formes héroïques de la vie*). "I wish to be read by men who remain children at any cost" (*Je souhaite d'être lu par personnes qui restent des enfants coûte que coûte*).[60] In his biographical sketch is his early recollection of the Comedie-Française, in anticipation of the "*trois coups funestes d'Oedipe-Roi*."[61] It is the "*sonnerie*" ("the alarum"), which the sphinx in the second act awaits so impatiently so she could be freed from waiting for a victim. There is no other treatment of the Oedipus-theme which would be so autobiographically interwoven with the life of the writer as that of Cocteau! Still, it is not with his own life sunk into the unconscious but with the life of the soul which knows no intellectual boundaries between the conscious and unconscious, between this side and that side, or autobiography and myth.

We read two decades later in Thomas Mann's *The Chosen One* (1951) words fundamental to Cocteau's Oedipus drama, which is essentially a Jocasta-drama, on the coherence of the conscious and unconscious soul. They are found in the confession of the Sibyl, i.e., a late Jocasta:

> For the soul is positioned on the surface, and there is much ado about the diabolical delusion which bewitches it. But deep below where the truth silently remains there are not any delusions given. On the contrary, it is there that

the sameness similar to the first glance has
been noted, and it unknowingly knowing has
taken man as its own child because it is again
the only one of equally high birth. There it is,
and with it the last is now being entered upon,
for it would be unworthy of the papal ear when
she does not confess the shifty nature of her
soul and holds back.

Whereupon even the pope, "The Chosen," can but
confess that "where the soul acts sensibly the child
likewise knew rightly that it was his mother whom
he loved."[62]

The soul knows everything. Only it cannot always
or does not always want to communicate its message.
In the spiritual first act, "The Phantom," the soul
of Laius would like to communicate, and it can,
too—to the watch-soldiers, childlike souls, as Cocteau's audience must be, but not to the prelate Teiresias or to Jocasta, who speaks French to royal personages with a strong international accent. Why
does she call Teiresias "Zizi"? Does she think
something has faded of the Kaiserin Elizabeth who
is called "Sisi" in the family and with whom as his
tragic heroine Cocteau was quite busy? But he most
assuredly saw Jocasta in the figure of Isadora Dun-
can and vice versa. He did this already in the celebrated tragic misfortune of the great dancer of
whom he writes in his memoirs, "This Jocasta . . .

victim of the complicity of a racing vehicle and a red shawl which hated her, threatened her, and warned her. Did she defy it and insist on wearing it?"[63] This happened in 1927. Had Cocteau at that time already named the one choked by the scarf Jocasta? The fatal sash, with which he introduced the queen and of which he lets it be said, "It will kill me!" he said for Isadora. No boundaries are allowed within the soul of the poet.

Nor within the soul of his Jocasta in the third act, "The Night of the Nuptials," a highpoint in the tradition of the Oedipus-theme. Herein Cocteau can be placed next to Hofmannsthal, not in the direction of *"sacralisation"* but neither in that of the *"désacralisation du mythe héroïque."*[64] Cocteau may have read Hofmannsthal's *Oedipus and the Sphinx* and found himself inspired by it in the second act. He belongs no less to the series of such "unsolemn" authors of the myth as Gide, Giraudoux, and Anouilh. At that highpoint in the third act he even constructs the polar opposite to Hofmannsthal, yet one equal in its depths. In Hofmannsthal this is the highest tension, an augmentation of the passion which cannot be outdone. In Cocteau it is the greatest relaxation and the relapse into the same place "where," in the words of Thomas Mann, "silently the truth lives" and "where the soul is not made a fool of." Cocteau's Jocasta does not conceal her amorous cravings for young men who are at the age of her son. Alone together in the wedding chamber, Oedipus and Jocasta both fall into a deep sleep, and for Oedipus the mother once again finds the cradle and lullaby before the great mirror, called "*psyche*" in French, the symbol of the spirits' haunt in which the "sameness"—this also Thomas Mann's word—of mother and wife is established at home.

What could follow as the fourth act, "Oedipus Rex," could thereupon be only a completely shortened version of Sophocles.

KARL KERÉNYI

5.

At the end of the path of *"désacralisation"* stands for
the time being—as well as temporarily, as also in
the sense of depleting every mythical sense—*A
Deserving Statesman* by T. S. Eliot (1959). The *sacrum,*
that ambivalence, has disappeared without a trace.
Remaining is only the appearance in itself, as
danger—through what means, one must ask?

Lord Cleverton, the last Oedipus not tainted with
any incest, is "gone through a door which we do not
see," from appearance into being. But since the consideration of incest was completely dispelled from
this Oedipus drama, what takes its place? A common but passionate youthful love-affair. The passing over of a corpse and the "driver-escape" take
the place of the father-murder. This motif turns out
to be so unimportant in the more recent history of
the theme; indeed more prominent was the *sacrum*
in the union with his mother. It is strange that, by
eliminating this motif, the love, now permitted insofar as passion is an issue, appears to one in her
position as that dangerous, great good, for which an
important poet with his transformed, creative depiction substitutes! Has that *sacrum* actually disappeared
without a trace—or must it hold its ground only
through a *substitute*? The idea in the depiction of the

poet is in fact this, that incest *can* be replaced through completely liberated love's passion—perhaps the deepest insight of Eliot in the piece! The words of the enamored Monica refer back into the depths where the myth reveals a loving Ur-goddess unlimited in its "sameness of the mother and goddess":

> Since the beginning of the world I have
>   loved you.
> Already before you and I were born, the love
> Which always brought us together was there.

Eliot is not the first to attempt to establish the Ur-love in the position of the Ur-mother as the Ur-loving. In a divine world Eros has his place as well—the Ur-love seen as a god. But whose love was the initial love in a world ruled by the immanent necessity of love and no longer ruled by the gods of the Greeks, as is the world of Eliot in this last Oedipus drama? What sort of being could there be at the beginning, if not a maternal one? Monica, since she has "loved since the beginning of the world," must now again recognize herself as such in her preexistent form.

1. Cf. my *The Heroes of the Greeks*,[2] trans. H. J. Rose (London: Thames and Hudson, 1974), 88–104 (and 391 ff.).

2. Hyginus *Fabulae* LCVII: *iratus inscius.*

3. *Oedipus Rex* 980–82.

4. *Odyssey* 11.271–80.

5. *Iliad* 23.679–80.

6. Ludwig Deubner, "Odipusprobleme," *Abhandlungen der Akad. Berlin* (1942): 38.

7. *Oedipus Rex* 58–61.

8. *Oedipus Rex* 1061.

9. Karl Reinhardt, *Sophokles*[3] (Frankfurt a. M., 1947), 104 ff.; Wolfgang Schadewaldt, *Hellas und Hesperien* (Zürich, 1960), 277 ff.

10. *Oedipus Rex* 189–92.

11. *Oedipus Rex* 1329–330.

12. *Pyth.* viii, 95/96.

13. Sigmund Freud, *Selbstdarstellung*[2] (1936), 89 ff.

14. Cf. my *Asklepios*, Bollingen Series (New York, 1959), 76 f.

15. Thucydides II, 54.

16. According to the ancient summary of the *Oedipus at Colonus.*

17. The Hungarian poet Michael Babits.

18. Cf. my *Eleusis*, Bollingen Series (New York, 1967), 84 ff.

19. Carl Robert, *Oidipus* (Berlin, 1915), 274.

20. Ibid., 6.

21. Ibid., 9.

22. See above, n. 18.

23. *Oedipus at Colonus* 1224–228.

24. *Oedipus at Colonus* 1627/8.

25. Sigmund Freud, *Vorlesungen zur Einführung in die Psychoanalyse*[2] (1922), 345 ff.

26. The main passage was restored by Carl Robert (above, n. 19), 315.

27. Carl Robert, 307 with ill. 48.

28. Tacitus *Annales* I, 62: *imperatorem . . . adtrectare feralia debuisse.*

29. 4 April 1717, quoted by Louis Moland in the preface to Voltaire's *Oeuvres complètes* II (1877).

30. In his *"examen"* to the piece.

31. Act I, scene i, at the end.

32. The final verse of the tragedy.

33. Hölderlin, *Sämtliche Werke* ("Grosse Stuttgarter Ausgabe"), V (1952), 450.

34. Quoted by W. Schadewaldt in his preface to *Sophokles, Tragödien* (Fisher Bücherei), 162, 14 and 25.

35. Wilhelm Dilthey, *Das Erlebnis und die Dichtung*,[4] 456.

36. Karl Reinhardt, *Tradition und Geist* (Göttingen, 1960), 382 and 386.

37. Hölderlin, *Sämtliche Werke* VI, 1 (1954), 434.

38. Ibid., 436.

39. Ibid. I, 1 (1946), 311; cf. W. Kirchner in *Hölderlin-Jahrbuch* (1951), 108.

40. Ibid., 70.

41. Ibid., 81.

42. Cf. above, n. 25.

43. Cf. above, nn. 7 and 8.

44. Karl Reinhardt, *Sophokles*[3] (Frankfurt a. M., 1947), 104.

45. L. 988, in the translation l. 1025.

46. W. Kirchner, *Der Hochverratsprozess gegen Sinclair* (Marburg/L., 1949), 63 ff.

47. Sigmund Freud, *Aus den Anfängen der Psychoanalyse, Briefe an Wilhelm Fliess, Abhandlungen und Notizen aus den Jahren 1887–1902* (Frankfurt a. M., 1950), 193.

48. Hofmannsthal, *Briefe 1900–1902*, no. 2.

49. Letter from 21 September 1904.

50. Cf. above, n. 49; for the date cf. W. Jens, *Hofmannsthal und die Griechen* (Tübingen, 1955), 91 ff.

51. Roger Martin du Gard, *Notes sur André Gide (1913–1951)* (Paris, 1951), 21.

52. André Gide, *Journal (1889–1939)*, 1151 (2 January 1933).

53. A. Szerb, *Die Suche nach dem Wunder* (Amsterdam-Leipzig, 1938), 60 f.

54. Act III (Dialogue with Creon).

55. Roger Martin du Gard, *Notes*, 22.

56. Cf. Helen Watson-Williams, *André Gide and the Greek Myth* (Oxford, 1967), 112.

57. Cf. quotation from an unpublished copybook of Gide in Watson-Williams, *Greek Myth*, 163, and her more detailed representation of Gide's ideas.

58. Cf. the final passage of Chapter I/4 and above, n. 24.

59. *Oedipe-Roi* (Paris, 1928), 2.

60. Jean Cocteau, *Essai* (Paris, 1932), ix; *Portrait-Souvenir 1900–1914* (Paris, 1935), 49.

61. *Portrait-Souvenir*, 23.

62. Thomas Mann, *Ges. Werke* VII (1960), 254–55.

63. *Portrait-Souvenir*, 152.

64. R. Trousson, *Le thème de Prométhée dans la littérature européenne* (Genf, 1964), 435, on Gide's *Le Prométhée mal enchaîné* (1899).

Oedipus Revisited

JAMES HILLMAN

1. Myth and Psychoanalysis

To take up the theme of Oedipus is a heroic engagement. Can you imagine the weight that falls when opening yet again the pages of Sophocles' play, the play that Aristotle used for explaining the nature of tragedy, that Freud used for explaining the nature of the human soul, the volume that drowned with Shelley off Lerici, a tale of a hero told by Homer and Aeschylus and Euripides as well, and retold by Seneca, Hölderlin, Hoffmansthal, Voltaire, Gide; and add to that the shelves of scholarly apparatus, interpretations, commentaries, arguments; and then, to bring this inhumanly heroic theme in public ostentation as a fifteenth contribution to our annual here*—the heroism, or *chutzpah*, is beyond all decent proportion.

*This essay was first composed and delivered as a lecture at the Eranos Conference, Ascona, Switzerland, August 1987.

So it is necessary before we begin to acknowledge a God in today's work, Apollo, and his hero, Oedipus, so that they do not devastate us with surprise. We confess at the outset to the lure of the Apollonic hero so as not to fall prey to the myth itself, to its self-blinding propensity, its badgering persistence to discover and expose, its patricidal impulse to kill old kings, and to its incestuous inflation that could produce as progeny yet another incestuously psychoanalytic paper on the Oedipus complex. By this opening propitiation, I beg that the myth not be mine. May Apollo stay distant as is his nature, as well Oedipus and Laius, and even Teiresias, and the ancestors Sophocles and Freud, too. Allow me to accord you reverence, yet kindly afford me safety from your sway while in your presence.

This gesture at the beginning is made in recognition of the power of myth. The *Wirksamkeit* of myth, its reality, resides precisely in its power to seize and influence our psychic life. The Greeks knew this so well, and so they had no depth psychology and psychopathology such as we have. They had myths. And we have no myths as such—instead, depth psychology and psychopathology. Therefore, as I have been repeating here fifteen times, psychology shows myths in modern dress and myths show our depth psychology in ancient dress.

The first to recognize this truth which is foundational for modern depth psychology was Sigmund

Freud. The first to recognize the implications of Sigmund Freud's recognition of the relation between myth and psyche, between antiquity and modern psychology, was C. G. Jung. Hear this passage which I have abbreviated from the opening page of Jung's pathbreaking work *Wandlungen und Symbole der Libido* (*Symbols of Transformation, CW* 5, §§1-2). Although this book was published in 1912, Jung retained this opening passage intact in his 1952 revision.

> Anyone who can read Freud's *Interpretation of Dreams*, . . . [and] can let this extraordinary book work upon his imagination calmly and without prejudice, will not fail to be deeply impressed at that point where Freud reminds us that an individual conflict, which he calls the incest fantasy, lies at the root of that monumental theme of the ancient world, the Oedipus legend. . . . we suddenly catch a glimpse of the simplicity and grandeur of the Oedipus tragedy, that perennial highlight of the Greek theater. This broadening of our vision has about it something of a revelation . . . when we follow the path traced out by Freud. . . . then the gulf that separates our age from antiquity is bridged over, and we realize with astonishment that Oedipus is still alive for us. . . . This truth opens the way to an understanding of the classical spirit such as has never existed before. . . .

> By penetrating into the blocked subterranean
> passages of our own psyches we grasp the liv-
> ing meaning of classical civilization, and at the
> same time . . . gain an objective understand-
> ing of [our own] foundations. That at least is
> the hope we draw from the rediscovery of the
> immortality of the Oedipus problem.

Now hear Freud's words:

> Falling in love with one parent and hating the
> other forms part of the permanent stock of the
> psychic impulses . . . of early childhood. . . .
> Antiquity has furnished us with legendary mat-
> ter which corroborates this belief, and the pro-
> found and universal validity of the old legends
> is explicable only by an equally universal valid-
> ity of the above-mentioned hypothesis regard-
> ing the psychology of children. I am referring
> to the. . . . *Oedipus Rex* of Sophocles.[1]

Freud recounts the plot, the *mythos*, briefly. Then he
says:

> The action of the play consists simply in the
> disclosure, approached step by step and artis-
> tically delayed (and comparable to the work of
> a psychoanalysis) that Oedipus himself is the
> murderer of Laius. . . .

This analogy between the poetic art and the artfulness of psychoanalysis Freud states again:

> As the poet, by unraveling the past, brings the guilt of Oedipus to light, he forces us to become aware of our own inner selves.

Then this:

> If *Oedipus Rex* moves a modern audience no less than it did the contemporary Greeks, the only possible explanation is that. . . . there must be a voice within us which is prepared to acknowledge the compelling power of fate in the *Oedipus.* . . . His fate moves us only because it might have been our own, because the oracle laid upon us before our birth the very curse which rested upon him.

These passages show that the particular myth uniting psychoanalysis with Greek antiquity is the *Oedipus Tyrannos* of Sophocles. It is therefore inescapable—please note my language already takes on the Oedipus vocabulary—if we would be faithful to the project of an archetypal re-visioning of depth psychology, that this Oedipus be revisited.

By an 'archetypal re-visioning' I mean tracing the imaginal roots that govern the ways psychology thinks and feels. I mean restoring behavior to its fictions, an *epistrophé* of life's blind enactments and sufferings called abnormal psychology, an imagining of our field and its work in terms of *archai, daimones,* and Gods. My project of imagining follows directly from Jung's most extraordinary and foundational statement, ontologically and methodologically foundational for whatever may justly be called "Jungian": "The psyche creates reality every day. The only expression I can use for this activity is *fantasy*. . . . Fantasy, therefore, seems to me the clearest expression of the specific activity of the psyche" (*CW* 6, *8*78).

I follow Jung here most assiduously, believing that psychology is truly psychological only when it awakens to the fantasies objectified in its observations. Analysts in practice are obliged to notice the fantasies we have in reading our patients: so, depth psychology is obliged to notice its fantasies in reading its theories. A psychology that observes, reports, formulates, and explains the patient, or the psyche in large, remains like the patient who observes, reports, and explains—that is, projective or, let us say, blind, not seeing the very eye it is seeing with. Hence, we turn to the bedrock of fantasies, the myths, for how else can psychology as it is now conceived awaken to itself.

The project of course has a heroic cast; for how imagine projects except as heroic projections, redemptive, culturally liberating, yet always in service to the founding fathers by continuing their line. The project would lift or deepen human life from its horizontal wanderings and labyrinthine riddlings always to something more-than-human, at times animal, at times alchemical, at times cultural, at times mythical. It would restore to insight its origins in the epiphanic, even theophanic, moment, authenticating interpretation with the truth of beauty and the sudden joy of recognition, truth and beauty as one. Indeed, the thrust is heroic because it is so fiercely anti-humanistic, as if parented by a divinity and with a desire to return all things to that divinity, yet just as equally heroic because the other parent is humanly mortal, naive, foolish, anchored in the ordinary world of community and *polis*.

So, we shall be continuing the line of Freud and Jung, drawing further parallels between myth and psychoanalysis. And we shall try to go beyond Freud's concentration on incest and parricide which narrowed his insight. Our first aim is to unearth other relevances for depth psychology in the Oedipus story, for that is where the theater of Oedipus continues to be performed.

2. *Family as Fate*

Freud has been attacked for reducing the noble Greek notion of heroic destiny to the banal intimacies of family. To Fliess, Freud wrote: "The Greek myth seizes on a compulsion which everyone recognizes because he has felt traces of it in himself. Every member of the audience was once a budding Oedipus in phantasy. . . ."[2] Moreover, detractors say, Freud got it completely wrong. He tells the tale so that the murder of the father results from desire for the mother. Whereas in play and legend, first came the murder and then the incest, and an incest without lust. Freud emphasized the mother, providing the ground for his materialist reductions. However, according to the legend, we fall into the arms of the mother only after killing the father: the seduction of *mater* and materialisms of whatever sort are consequent to the murder of the unknown father. When we kill the father we are Oedipus.

Who, what, where is this unknown father in actual psychology? I have to assume that any contrary spirit that cannot be evaded may be an unrecognized father. Do we not meet a 'father' in those moments of obstruction which narrow the path to singlemindedness, those moments of resistance when we will

not give way to what crosses us? Jung once defined
God with these words:

> To this day God is the name by which I des-
> ignate all things which cross my wilful path
> violently and recklessly, all things which upset
> my subjective views, plans and intentions and
> change the course of my life for better or
> worse.[3]

By resisting the unknown that crosses "my subjective views, plans and intentions," I kill the father. I
do not let myself be moved by the chance spirit
which blows for ill or good, or both. Resistance is
indeed central to analysis, for it is essential to Oedipus's heroic style. Yet, at the same time, this style ac-
cords a fathering power to the other, unconsciously
acknowledging that the other crossing my way has
the fathering power to change my life. It is my King.
The other's great 'No' fathers me by standing in my
way. *Eris, polemos*, strife, war, said Heraclitus, is the
father of all things.

The critics also say, because of Freud, every family
reduces to the single same account, a monomyth,
and myth itself reduces to compulsions and repres-
sions derived from family. The battles with cosmic
fate become the repression of desires. A human life
is not called by fate, but compelled by desire. The

tragic hero Oedipus becomes Little Hans with a phobia. And the Oedipus which is in us all becomes a five-year-old child, a little bud of lust and murder. And what a curse Freud put on family life. "I will never come near my parents," swears Oedipus (Grene, 1007)—separation, suspicion, ignorance, abandonment, incest, infanticide, suicide, mutilation, and cursing into the next generation when old Oedipus at Colonus turns his wrathful back on his fighting sons.

Of course Freud got it wrong—but I am not joining with his critics. Freud 'got it wrong,' because it is the genius of psychology to get it wrong, to disturb, pervert, dislocate, misread, so as to lift the repression of the usual sense. Psychoanalysis goes wrong in order to keep close to the wrongness in the case, whatever the case may be. Pathologizing is homeopathic: like cures like. There must be madness in the method if the method would reach the madness.

Besides, there are other ways of reading Freud. Yes, he did secularize fate into ordinary family emotion and cast his dark pathologized eye on family phenomena. Yet Freud ennobled family with a mythical dimension, for his pathologized view was at the same time a mythologized view, confirming once more the root metaphor of depth psychology: mythology presents pathology; pathology, mythology. We require both to grasp either.

The infusion of Greek myth into the medical, academic, commercial, and often Jewish Vienna of the 1890s—Freud's world and the world of his clientele—brought to family a transparency beyond bourgeois materialism and its hysteria. While Oedipus collapses into Hansi down the street, there glimmers through little Hans the radiance of Oedipus, Sophocles, Greece, and the Gods. As Freud says: "Hans was really a little Oedipus who wanted to have his father out of the way, to get rid of him, so that he might be alone with his handsome mother and sleep with her."[4] *Really*, that is Freud's word. What is *really* at work in the case is myth; what is really going on in family is myth: to feel myth in the daily world, just stay home with the family. Of course, it drives one crazy.

By returning family back to mythical figures, Freud performed an *epistrophé*. He reimagined our desires, our phobias, our childhoods. He relocated the human world in the mythical imagination. The World Parents of creation myths became the parental world: the parental world became our culture's creation myth, at once personal, secular, and historical. Parents gain supreme authority in the generation of the psychic cosmos. Whether actual, whether imagos, whether archetypal Mother and Father, parents become the great dominants. A father's terrifying authority arises—not because of introjected conventional religion which Freud abjured or because of patriarchal social norms—but because of myth: in the father is Laius and Apollo and the myth embroiling Laius, and in the mother is the Queen, the throne, the city.

Ever since, psychoanalysis performs this *epistrophé*—if we read it in this light. Ever since, psychoanalysts are the myth-preservers in our culture. They go on ritualizing the Oedipal tale, go on affirming the cosmic power of parents and childhood for discovering identity. By divinizing the parental world, each patient discovers a budding Oedipus in the soul. We believe we are what we are because of our childhoods in family, but this only because the actual family is "really" Oedipal—that is, mythical. Even as actual, sociological, statistical family life dissolves, psychoanalysis retains the myth. Early years and repressed memories are so fateful, in our culture, because psychoanalysis dominates our cult of souls and Oedipus is the dominant myth practiced in the cult. Depth psychology believes in myth, practices myth, teaches myth. That myth hides from recognition and lies disguised in literal and secular case histories is appropriate to the very myth they teach—the tale of Oedipus, its disguises and pursuit of self-recognition.

We must see this clearly, and here again I use Oedipal heroic language. The fact that literal family holds such sway in analytic considerations is because we are each "really Oedipus," and this not because our psyches want our mothers but because we are, in soul, mythical beings. We emerge into life as creatures in a drama, scripted by the great storytellers of our culture. And as budding Oedipus we immediately transpose the stock figures of Mom and Dad, or the absent Mom or Dad as is mainly the situation today, or aunt or stepfather or daycare lady—whoever plays their stand-ins—into Jocasta and Laius, ennobling desire, parents, memory, forgetting, foretelling, early family scenes, early abandonments, abuses and mutilations, little boy and little girl wishes, and endowing these small, pre-initiatory events with salient inevitable determinacy.

But none of this is literal. We must see this clearly: none of it can be taken at only this one level of historical fact. Not what happened in childhood, not your recollections of lust and hatred, not even what is recalled or not recalled but buried, nor your parents as such—all these emotions and configurations are ways in which we are remythologized. And that is why these emotions and configurations carry such importance. They are doors to Sophocles and Sophocles himself a door. Their importance rises not from historical events but by mythical happenings that, as Sallustius said, never happened but always are, as fictions.[5]

For the same reason Freud's basic theory still dominates—and will. It too is myth, wearing the costume appropriate to the *nigredo* consciousness of science's materialism. What holds us to Freud, provoking countless retellings and commentaries such as this one now, is not the science in the theory but the myth in the science. Freud wrote to Einstein in 1932:

> It may perhaps seem to you as though our theories are a kind of mythology and, in the present case, not even an agreeable one. But does not every science come in the end to a kind of mythology like this? Cannot the same be said today of your own Physics? (*SE* 22: 211)

Individual patients struggling with self-knowledge are so convinced by the fictions of childhood because they are Oedipus, who finds who he is by finding out about his infancy, its wounds and abandonment. The entire massive apparatus of counseling, social work, developmental psychology—therapy in every form—continues rehearsing the myth, practicing the play in its practices.

3. Sick City

Freud is little concerned with the relation between the tragedy of Oedipus and the tragedy of the city. For Sophocles, *polis* is central to the play. The play is filled with longing to find the father and to cure the city. The mysteries of parricide and of the *polis* are inseparable. Only that resolution which cures the city can satisfy. For Oedipus—or any one of us —to find one's father and the truth of oneself is not enough, because there is a murder in the order of the world, and the world and the soul are inseparable. That is why the longing in the play is so intense: the world must be restored, not only its men and women. So the play is called *Oedipus Tyrannos*: Oedipus, ruler of the city, rex, king.

The play opens with the presenting complaints of a sick city. A priest of Zeus appeals to Oedipus:

The city, as you see, wastes in blight,
Blight on earth's fruitful blooms and grazing flocks,
And on the barren birth pangs of the women.
The fever God has fallen on the city,
And drives it, a most hated pestilence. . . .[6]

Oedipus replies:

I am not ignorant
. . . Well I know
You are all sick, and in your sickness none
There is among you as sick as I,
For your pain comes to one man alone,
To him and to none other, but my soul [*psychē*]
Groans for the state, for myself, and for you.
. . . .
Know that already I have
. . . .
. . . sought, and found one remedy . . .

(Cook, 60–69)

The King has taken on the city and its people as himself. He calls them his children, *tekna*. He identifies his condition with theirs. He *is* the city and its people. We are dealing, however, with something beyond the symbolic significance of kingship, and rather with the interpenetration of sickness among the *polis*, its people, and the individual. All are sick together: individuals, community, and government. Private and public cannot be separated. The Gods do not affect individuals and families alone or only human beings: they affect the land, the crops and herds, the institutions of state. A city, too, can be pathologized by mythical factors—exactly what Jung said in *Wotan* in 1936.[7] The Gods live in the *polis*.

Depth psychology has drawn conclusions from the play about the suffering of soul in the family. Depth

psychology can draw further conclusions about the
suffering of soul, psychopathology, in the city. How
does a city act when it is sick? What moves do its
rulers make? What notions of remedy arise from a
sick city?

First, the sick city calls upon the leader to find
remedy, equating King with City, Oedipus Tyrannos.
The government is responsible. The people are
children.

Second, the leader calls on Apollo to reveal the
cause and the cure:

> And this I did . . .
> Creon, my brother-in-law, I sent away
> Unto Apollo's Pythian halls to find
> What I might do or say to save the state [*polis*].
>   (Cook, 70–73)

The government turns to Apollonic consciousness,
Apollonic means of diagnosis and correction. And
the government speaks in God's name: "God proclaimed now to me. . . . For me, and God, and for
our land" (244–54).

Third, the sick city summons the seer, shaman,
or prophet for clearly seeing the nature of the ills.
Oedipus sends for Teiresias, because "what [he] sees,
is most often what the Lord Apollo sees" (Grene,
285–87).

Fourth, the city purges. Oedipus says, "I will

JAMES HILLMAN

disperse this filth" (Cook, 138). Creon says: "Lord
Phoebus clearly bids us to drive out . . . a pollution
we have nourished in our land" (Cook, 97–99). Oedipus speaks of purification, expulsion, punishment;
he curses those who would not obey him. As there
is one remedy, the oracle of Apollo, so there is one
villain, the scapegoat murderer. Creon, returning
from the Pythian oracle, speaks of robbers in the
plural (123), and Oedipus in the next speech con-
tracts the plural to the singular. The indefinite plural
"murderers" become the single scapegoat on whom
all blame shall fall:

> I forbid that man, whoever he may be, my land,
> . . . and I forbid any to welcome him
> or cry him greeting or make him a sharer
> in sacrifice or offering to the Gods
> or give him water for his hands to wash.
> I command all to drive him from their homes
> since he is our pollution.
>
> (Grene, 236–43)

Fifth, the sick city makes edicts. Oedipus says: I
forbid, I command, I invoke this curse. In these early
passages of the play, he speaks as the voice of the
city, whereas Teiresias uses *ego* eight times in their
exchange, referring to himself as a person.[8] Oedipus
Tyrannos is the state, an utterly public figure: *l'état
c'est moi.*

These five solutions—and let me repeat them *en bref*: a single answer to a complex problem, the appeal to Apollo, the reliance upon the prophetic seer, the language of pollution and expulsion, and apodictic declarations in God's Name—these supposed solutions are actually manifestations of the city's sickness. They are diagnostic signs. The solutions imagined by a patient for his illness belong to the image of the illness. That is why therapists listen closely to what the patient wants at the beginning of therapy. How the patient imagines remedy and what measures he is already pursuing show how the patient is constellated by his condition. The *solutions* to the problem of Thebes present the *problem* of Thebes. The city suffers because of Oedipus, of course. Every playgoer knows that.

The city suffers more profoundly, however, from the Apollonic way in which it reflects on its suffering. Oedipus is the scapegoat, because the city imagines itself in the manner of expelling evil. And it finds the scapegoat as prophesied because its consciousness fulfills its prophetic structure. "Phoebus who proposed the riddle, himself/Should give the answer—who the murderer was," says the Chorus (Storr, 279).

The Chorus, however, does not altogether follow the Apollonic mode; the Chorus extends the divine background. It mentions Zeus, Fates (*keres*), nymphs, Pegasus. It refers the pestilence to Ares (1911) and calls on Athene (158), Artemis (161), and Dionysos (212) for protection, even suggesting for Oedipus fathering Gods other than Apollo: Pan, Hermes, Dionysos. So, the Chorus embraces a vision wider than an Apollonic notion of government and cures for its ills. The city is sick. "Shipwreck" is the term: the marketplace in turmoil, the youth in the streets, the crops, the herds, the women barren, to all of which there is one appeal and one solution, according to the Oedipal and Apollonic mode: "Lay on the King" (*Henry V*, 4, 1).

There could be other ways than the five measures we have just specified. If we listen to the Chorus, then we would look for the other remedies backed by other Gods. When the institutions of the state are in shipwreck, then turn to the institutions themselves. If the crops, then why not a Demeterian remedy; if the women, then the protections of the marriage bed and childbirth. Concrete measures conceived in response to concrete cases. A differentiation of the single illness according to its multiple manifestations. This pragmatic, non-heroic approach is much as in a modern city: the problems reside not just in City Hall or the White House. Kicking out the King will not change the school system or the high cost of highway repair. But: alter the architecture, the water works, the marketplaces, the child care, the traffic patterns—and the city itself changes. Healing takes place without a master plan or edicts from above but by honoring the varieties of Gods in the specific concrete places of their presences.

4. *Identity and Landscape*

Oedipus is born in Thebes of his natural parents, Jocasta and Laius. He is raised in Corinth by his foster parents, Merope and Polybus. But his native land is neither, since he is expelled from the home of Thebes and leaves the home of Corinth. His landscape is in-between. The in-between place appears in the story as the crossroads that is neither Thebes nor Corinth, and the in-between place appears also as the landscape of Mt. Cithaeron. The Theban shepherd takes the infant Oedipus to this mountain, where he is rescued by the Corinthian shepherd. The Chorus, addressing Cithaeron, calls Oedipus a "native of your land" (Cook, 1093); Cithaeron is his "nurse and mother" (1094). Teiresias predicts that this mothering mountain shall provide no harbor, offer no corner for his cries when Oedipus is blind and in exile (421). Aeschylus says blind old Oedipus wandered the mountain. Natives there were said to show a spot that, following the text (1455), is his grave. Oedipus himself says, near the end of the play: "Cithaeron, why did you receive me?" (Grene, 1391), then turning to it finally: "Leave me live/in the mountains where Cithaeron is, that's called/*my* mountain. . ." (Grene, 1452–454).

What is Cithaeron? Why there his home, his infancy, his despair, his grave? What has that landscape to say about Oedipus, and what does "my" landscape say about any human nature?

There are many stories told of the mountain by mythographers from Pausanias through Kerényi — and it is appropriate to mention here again the extraordinary service Kerényi performed, collecting the tales and their depictions on vases and graves and retelling the stories. Cithaeron is a wild place, a killing field, rugged and rocky, though rich, moist, and grassy on its lower slopes.[9] The lion that Hercules first killed and whose skin he wore may have come from here. Teiresias saw the coupling snakes on Cithaeron, killing one, and was cursed to lose his sight therefore. Another murderous snake story says the mountain is named for a youth who rejected the seductive appeal of the Fate Tisiphone — a fate who instigates men to kill each other.[10] She killed him with one of her poisonous serpentine hairs. Babies were exposed on Cithaeron — for instance, Antiope's twin sons. Other brothers with brutal histories gave names to this pair of mountains: Cithaeron and Helikon. Cithaeron, envious and greedy of his father's domain, pushed his father off the mountain, and then he too fell from the same cliff. Or, the brothers killed each other; and Helikon, the mild one, gave his name to the brother mountain inhabited by the Muses. Deep incestuous passions haunt this earth: Zeus and Hera there consummated that sacred, and incestuous, wedding. On this mountain Pentheus followed the troop of Dionysos, and there, on Cithaeron, he was torn apart by the Maenads, among whom was his mother. Deep passions, killing fields, madness.

Concerning this madness: "On one peak of Cithaeron," says Plutarch (*Aristides* 11), "is the cave of the Sphragitidian nymphs . . . and many of the natives were possessed, . . . *nympholepti* ('seized by the nymphs')." Frazer comments on the passage, saying that the nymphs were mischievous at noon, especially at summer noon.[11] The places of great danger, of being seized by nymphs and so made mad, were wells, springs, rivers, shadow of trees, and "at cross roads for these places are [their] mid-day haunts . . . and a man who lingers there may be struck by a nymph, the consequences of which would be some mental or bodily ailment, generally the loss of reason. . . ." Frazer goes on, referring to another sanctuary of nymphs where "to cure such cases it is customary to prepare and place at a spot where three roads meet (*tristrata*) . . . some bread . . . honey, milk, and eggs to appease these nymphs."

The plot thickens: as with Sophocles' play or Freudian analysis, we begin to detect a repressed or forgotten clue. Again the Oedipal imagination catches us in its atmosphere. Our very way of pursuing the topic seeks to bring to light the buried "real story." And the clues are so evident, for Laius's route lay hard by Mt. Cithaeron: "a narrow cross road between Kithairon and Potniai," says Kerényi.[12] Neither would give way; a violent fight; son kills father. The place is several times called a "triple way." As to the time of day the men met, the play does not say. But Phoebus Apollo, the bright solar God, is its tutelary spirit throughout; the entire drama is under the blaze of noon when nymphs are most dangerous.

No appeasing bread, honey, milk, or eggs, no soul food, at this crossroads. What sudden madness, what "loss of reason," overcame them? Was it nympholepsy? Did the nymph of the place seize the two men, so much alike as Jocasta says (743): the elder one, Laius, sterile, who had repeatedly been to the oracle to request a child and then, siring one, orders him slain, and who has taken another man's son as his lover—of which we shall have more to say. And the other man, Oedipus, who had overcome the Sphinx with his "wit" as he says (397), solved the *ainigma* as a riddle, a problem—hey, no problem—not ever seeing, as Jung[13] says, that she herself was the problem, not ever seeing the monstrosity, having so very little wit that he hears no warnings, lives, and breeds with his mother without ever seeing, without ever knowing.

Were they both, father and son, susceptible to nympholepsy, to noon's shadow, that high solar madness called *superbia*, a soullessness or absence of anima, psychologically inept? Like the play and like an analytical session: we shall have to postpone the dénouement of this anima question until the end of our analysis.

Besides this particular theme of the nymphs and the anima, there is a wider inference to draw. The nymph who strikes is the mood of a place, the face and form of a landscape. Gestalt psychology calls this embodiment of mood in a geography its "physiognomic character."[14] An actual physical setting—well, spring, tree, crossroads—is animated; the airs, waters, places are ensouled. Our souls on earth receive the earth in our souls, an idea once expressed as the individuating effect of matter.[15] Oedipus of Thebes and Corinth and Colonus is also of, mainly of, Cithaeron. Do we not learn something more from Sophocles than Freud transmitted? Is there not a shaping of human natures, and thus our human destinies, by the shape of the nature in which we live? Geography too parents us. Freud (*SE* 19: 178) rewrote Napoleon so as to say "Anatomy is Destiny"; but Napoleon's original, "Geography is Destiny," is today more psychological. What we do for and with and to this nature, how we live our ecological life, affects the soul's animal, vegetative, and mineral substance. Ecological life is also psychological life. And if ecology is also psychology, then "Know Thyself" is not possible apart from knowing thy world.

5. *Laius, Infanticide, and Literalism*

Freud says "the oracle laid upon us before our birth the very curse which rested upon him." The Oedipus complex pre-exists our birth. I suppose Freud to mean it is archetypal. In Oedipus's own case a curse was already on his father, Laius, that he would be killed by his son. The tragic career that leads Oedipus and Laius to the crossroads and the subsequent tragedies to all—Jocasta, their sons, Creon, Thebes—begin in the father's fear he will be killed by his son. So, Laius, to avoid the oracle, pinions the boy-child's feet, and he is exposed on Cithaeron (717). To save his own life, Laius orders his son's death. The plot begins in infanticide. Parricide is a consequent. In fact, Oedipus left Corinth so as not to kill his father.

But Laius wished to kill, tried to kill his son. Freud emphasizes parricide, both in regard to the Oedipal urge and to the primal horde, where sons kill the father. He says less about infanticide, about fathers killing sons. This desire in the father to kill the child we ignore to our peril, especially since psychoanalysis descends from fathers. If this myth is foundational to depth psychology, then infanticide is basic to our practice and our thought. Our practice and our thought recognize infanticide in the archetypal mother, its desire to smother, dissolve, mourn, bewitch, poison, and petrify. We are aware that inherent to mothering is 'bad' mothering. Fathering too is impelled by its archetypal necessity to isolate, ignore, neglect, abandon, expose, disavow, devour, enslave, sell, maim, betray the son—motifs we find in biblical and Hellenic myths as well as folklore, fairytales, and cultural history. The murderous father is essential to fathering, as Adolf Guggenbühl has written.[16] The cry to be fathered so common in psychological practice, as well as the resentment against the cruel or insufficient father so common in feminism—whether as cruel or insufficient ruler, teacher, analyst, institution, program, corporation, patriarchy, or God—idealizes the archetype. The cry and the resentment fail to recognize that these shadow traits against which the son protests are precisely those that initiate fathering.

This because: first, they kill idealization. The destructive father destroys the idealized image of himself. He smashes the son's idolatry. Whenever, wherever we idealize the father, we remain in sonship, in the false security of a good ideal. A good model, whether kind analyst, wise guru, generous teacher, honest chief, holds these virtues of kindness, wisdom, generosity, and honesty fixed in another, projected outside. Then, instead of initiation, imitation.[17] Then the son remains tied to the persons of the idealized figure. Keats, whose father died when

the boy was eight, said that he who would create—
let us say 'father'—must create or father himself. This
seems to happen naturally, for the broken ideal does
not simply disappear. It lives on like an aura, like
an inspiration rising up from mourning the father's
corpse. He is gone. He never really was; or, he was
rotten. The *putrefactio* of the idealized image experienced as mourning the father begins early and
continues long, because it is essential to the initiation of idealizing child into man of ideals. For the
ideals return, released from imprisonment in idealizations of a father image, settling down in the work
of life or the life of work. They begin to be realized
in those fathering acts that Keats called "soul-
making,"[18] and the *opus* becomes father, teacher,
master.

Second, the terrible traits in the father also initiate the son into the hard lines of his own shadow.
The pain of his father's failings teaches him that fail-
ing belongs to fathering. The very failure fathers the
son's failings. The son does not have to hide his share
of darkness. He grows up under a broken roof which
nonetheless shelters his own failings, inviting him,
forcing him, to be dark himself in order to survive.
The commonality—and commonness—of shared
shadow can bond father and son in dark and silent
empathy as deep as any idealized companionship.

Third, the terrible traits in the father provide a
counter-education.[19] How better bring home a true

appreciation of decency, loyalty, generosity, succor, and straightness of heart than by their absence or perversion? How more effectively awaken moral resolve than by provoking moral outrage at the father's bad example?

The prophecy before the birth of Oedipus states the result of Laius's attempt to avoid the prophecy. Taking action to avoid the prophecy fulfills the prophecy. Hence the feeling that oracles are inescapable, foredooming. But the doom is not in the prophecy; it is in the action taken when one hears the oracle literally. Laius hears literally and so literally tries to kill his son; so that literally he is killed by his son. Laius is cursed not by the oracle but by the literalism of archetypal pronouncements—a topic we discussed here two years ago regarding paranoia. Prophecy is a "forthtelling" (to use David Miller's term) stating in dark speech what is archetypally present as a dark potential and which *may* become acted in the day world in time. Only then does forthtelling become foretelling.

By this I am not saying what Laius should have done. We do not read a myth to correct it, to fault its figures. We read a myth to learn what it tells about psychic figuring, how the psyche configurates, figures out patterns of life. We read Oedipus to learn what it is to be a killer, not only of one's father but also, because of Laius, of one's son. We read Oedipus also to grasp something of the relation between what

Sophocles calls a bad, ugly, or evil oracle—the literal understanding of an oracle—and the killing.

The myth is replete with oracles, even depends on oracles for its tragedy. First, the oracle to which Laius went several times so as to have a son, then the oracle to which Creon goes to find what is wrong with the city; then there is the Sphinx, and Teiresias. How do oracles fit into the tragedy? Why do oracles belong to the action of the *Oedipus*?

Therapists often listen to dreams as oracles and turn for predictions to horoscopes, Tarot, and *I-Ching*. They want to caution a patient (supplicant) from a course that they predict will otherwise blindly lead to tragedy. This oracular way of hearing may indicate neither the therapist's shamanistic insight nor his practical perspicacity, nor even a Jungian belief in the unconscious. Rather, it may be showing the undying effect of Oedipus upon analysis. With Oedipus come the foreboding feelings of tragedy and the searching blindness, the blind search, for a way out. I will kill the father; so I'll get out of Corinth. The city is sick; so I'll drive out the culprit. In the heroic ear, the message is clear. Apollonic clarity. Apollonic oracles, Apollonic anxieties. The oracular approach would ward off with its literalism the tragedy that its literalism predicts. That is, the oracular approach to the psyche defends against its measureless depths (Heraclitus) with literalist measures. Because the forebodings of incurable tragedy—suicide, homicide, psychosis, cancer, etc.—that arise during an analysis belong to its myth, these fantasies remain an inherent part of its feeling. They are themselves incurable because they reflect the tragedy in its depths. Both Freud and Jung remained true to this tragic sense. Neither attempted to cure analysis of its tragic component. They incorporated the telling into their theory—theory as therapeutic because it embraces tragedy whether as shadow and evil (Jung) or as the fore-ordained and inescapable Oedipal complex itself.

Laius and Oedipus share more than Jocasta and the throne of Thebes. Father and son share a literalist psychology. (Jocasta says Oedipus resembles his father—774.) This is why they must oracularly meet at the crossroads and act the oracle literally. Both take oracles literally: the father abandons his son; the son flees from his assumed father (Polybus). Both actions aim not to fulfill the oracle; yet thereby they rush headlong into fulfilling it. Neither reflects the darkness in divine speech. They hear language in the same straight way. They are locked in tragedy and act the darkness as if both heroes were missing anima, unaffected by psychology, by which I mean Greek psychology in the tradition of Heraclitus who says how to read and hear oracles.[20]

Oedipus had an early chance with the Sphinx to practice the psychological ear. He heard the Sphinx, however, as a riddle, setting him a problem. He heard with a heroic ear. "I stopped her mouth" (Storr, 397). "I solved the riddle by my wit alone" (Grene, 398). In this passage, he intensifies his heroic stance by speaking of himself—until then rarely in the text—as *ego*.[21] Stopping the mouth of the Sphinx, another way of stopping his own ears, is the signal deed for which the Chorus praises him in the last verses of the play: ". . . behold this Oedipus,/Who solved the famous riddle [*ainigma*], was your mightiest man" (Cook, 1525). For the mightiest man, an enigma becomes a problem to be solved, vanquished. Yet an *ainigma*, as Marie Delcourt notes, refers to "*all things with a second sense*: symbols, oracles, Pythagorean wise-sayings. . . ."[22] An enigma is like a mantra or a koan or a Heraclitean gnomon to carry with one and learn from, Sphinx as emblem on a gemstone or mounted upon a pillar to be regarded, not shattered at the bottom of a cliff.

Commentators often point out that Oedipus did not hear Jocasta, Teiresias, or the herdsman warning him to leave off his singleminded pursuit. More important, Vernant says he did not hear "the secret discourse . . . at the heart of his own discourse."[23] *That* is his tragedy: not hearing the second sense— literalism. Perhaps literalism is at the heart of tragedy itself. "No literary genre in antiquity, in fact, uses so abundantly as tragedy expressions of double meaning, and *Oedipus Rex* includes more than twice as many ambiguous forms as the other plays of Sophocles."[24] Ricoeur says, ". . . Sophocles' tragedy reveals, . . . in the work of art itself, the profound unity of disguise and disclosure. . . ."[25] The hero hears only half, intolerant of ambiguity. He takes disguise literally as concealment and so insists upon literal disclosure as revelation.

Oedipus did have a second ear which opens after blinding at Colonus. But already in the *Tyrannos* he can hear otherwise. Right in the mathematical middle of the text, at its hinge, Oedipus tells that back in Corinth "a curious chance befell me . . . curious indeed. . . . There was a dinner and at it a drunken man accused me in his drink of being a bastard . . . this thing rankled always" (Cook/Grene, 776–86). He had begun to hear of himself differently, and it goes on echoing. An ambiguous Dionysian element is at work unconsciously. Much as it was at his conception; for let us remember, Laius conceived Oedipus at night while drunk. There is another fathering spirit in Oedipus's nature like the mothering mountain Cithaeron, a Dionysian place too, which resonates within and undoes the relentless course of his heroism.

If we imagine a second sense in the oracle, then Laius might have heard: "Watch your son deeply, study his heart, grasp his ways, for he has the potential for your end. He is the one who can show how your life ends, the ends of your life." The son offers another way than the father's. The son is the ruling mind's potential for a second sense. He *is* the next generation, a generative understanding beyond the literalism of a king's kind of consciousness, which hardens into single meanings when the bounds of any kingdom are defined, uniting into one dominion land, state, people, king: *tyrannos*. The tyranny of unity.

So, Laius puts the son away, as Sophocles phrases it. Oedipus put the Sphinx away too, for that's what heroes do. They take action against the curses, monsters, evils that are necessary for their action. What's a hero without an evil empire to oppose? Curses, monsters, evils become "problems" which have no second sense. But there is no "away," no permanent place to put a psychic content, as Freud said. The repressed returns—in this case from that murderous *topos* Cithaeron, the unconscious as a landscape of killing. Oedipus returns to kill the father who intended to kill him, even though Oedipus says (Grene, 1001), "I did not wish to kill my father." This Laius could not have said about his wish toward his son. In both cases, wishes and intentions are irrelevant. Tragedy comes from oracular literalism and the literal flight from it. Oracular literalism, heroic action, and tragedy twist into one knot.

The two ways—the father's and the son's—come together at the crossroads. The text uses the word "triple" for this place (716, 730, 800, 1399–1401). Three. Not opposite roads at cross purposes but triple, several paths, various senses of direction, as the French: *sens, sentier*. This crossroads, this metaphorical place, could be the place of metaphor, generative of *various* senses of direction, ways to go, ways to be, a crossing into a symbolic, gnomic darkening of understanding, even a way below to Hecate's mystification. But Laius and Oedipus, and the play, belong to heroic tragedy—particularly to Phoebus Apollo. Apollo as raven, wolf, and killer is not seen or heard in the sunlight of heroic action. The crossroads narrows into opposites and the literal darkness of blinding.

If Oedipus is our myth, analysts cannot be wary enough about reading dreams as foretellings and counseling actions from them. Just when we seem most on the track of clearing riddles we may be on the road of tragedy. The conversations in analysis are always more than secular. There is a further sense, once called anagogic, in every analytical utterance, because Freud brought in myth and myth brings in Gods. Each time we read literally in an oracular way, attempting to do Hermes' job of connecting worlds (and Hermes is not an oracular God)—whether we call these worlds life and dream, inner and outer, objective and subjective, psyche and reality—we follow Laius. We have lost the second sense in the literalism of the attempt. Hermes makes the connection; and hidden connections, as Heraclitus said, are the best. The clear, unambiguous connection may kill the child, the next generation.

I am proposing that infanticide is a mythic manner of imagining literalism. I am elaborating further an equation offered at Eranos in 1971: archetypal child personifies imagination. If infanticide means killing the second sense, then infanticide is the mythical equivalent of literalism. This further implies that literalism, when it is the father's desire to kill the child, is the semantic equivalent of the father–son conflict. The father–son conflict, discovered in myths the world over and often presented as the key to *Oedipus Rex* itself, is not its tragic *arché*. Rather, the father–son conflict will be seen as the root when we stay Oedipal in our imagination, assuming all things start in family. *Prior to that conflict is Oedipal discourse that does not hear into its own speech.* A literal discourse, a single meaningness would do away with the ambiguity that necessarily arises when sharing a kingdom with the next generation.

To go yet further: as I discussed at Eranos in 1973 regarding Hercules and the Underworld, literalism accompanies heroic action. Because the hero begins often as an object of infanticide, as an abandoned, endangered infant, the repression of the second sense is how heroism begins. Therefore, our culture's current focus on abandoned, exposed children is but another part of our culture's heroism.

I am suggesting that heroism forms discourse itself, not merely with verbs of action or muscular prose, but as a literalistic opposing sense. The second sense, when abandoned by the first, is now single and itself becomes literal. The second sense then returns from repression as a literal opponent to the ruling meaning, rather than as the son renewing the realm with connotative extensions.

Myths take place in discourse. They are enacted in how we speak. Is that not what the very word *mythos* implies? Alchemy knew this. The motif of king-and-king's-son plays there such a part, for without the second sense alchemy itself would perish. None of alchemy has only one sense: it cannot be read literally. So the conjunction of Rex and Regina, the *opus major*, depends on the prior cohesion of king-and-king's-son.[26] We hear alchemy with the metaphorical ears of a bearded Rex who is also a beardless *filius philosophorum*. Otherwise, alchemy literalizes into either primitive chemistry or spiritual magic.

The infanticide, the desire to kill the next generation, explains something of Laius's history previous to our text. Aeschylus named the first of his Oedipus tetralogy *Laius* (ca. 467 B.C.), and Euripides produced a *Laius* (ca. 411–09 B.C.). Neither is extant, though they are said to tell that Laius fell in love with the ravishing beauty of the son of King Pelops, the lad Chrysippos, and abducted him to be his lover. To Laius is attributed the first homosexual ravishment. He is called the inventor of pederasty[27] in the tradition of assigning the origin of a human trait, skill, or natural product to a God, a legendary figure, or community; that is, all things have an imaginal source in archetypal personifications. As punishment for this abduction, the oracle, or Pelops, cursed Laius to be killed by his own son.

Laius loved a boy and tried to kill his own boy. He could not generate, which was his reason for going to the oracle and for hearing it literally. His kingdom was barren already before Oedipus, before the Sphinx. Freud says boys want to be love objects of their fathers—a desire appearing in the clinical complaint and resentment we spoke of earlier: 'my father didn't love me.' Plato's dialogue *Laches*, a "dialogue in which fathers consult Socrates about the education of their sons," reports (180b) that "everyone who is occupied with public affairs . . . [is] apt to be negligent and careless of their own children."[28]

Fathers neglect their sons, do not fulfill the erotic bond, because—of the incest taboo.[29] Fathers like Laius hear the taboo only literally and so may love only other men's sons. Greek education notoriously so tied with Greek love portrays fathers loving other men's sons. As Eva Keuls writes: "The archetypal homosexual relationship was that between a childlike . . . boy and a mature man. The contact had strong paternal overtones. . . ."[30] If Laius is cursed for pederasty, his abducting Chrysippos from Pelops, this pederasty results from his literalism. *He hears the prohibition against incest as a prohibition against eros.*[31] The repressed returns as homoeros.

The father may not, dare not, cannot love his own son as his son would ideally be loved—not only because of the incest taboo, not only because of the public preoccupation of fathers as the *Laches* says, not only because the second sense is death to the tyrannic king. There is yet another reason shown by Laius. In fathering lurks infanticide. The father avoids or neglects his son because of the archetypal urge to kill him. If Oedipus is our myth, then Laius plays a part in it: to come close in love between fathers and sons also brings murder near. That cry for father, for a first principle, a creation myth, a roof that guarantees, an altar with sustaining presence, a base, a rock, pillar, platform, sheltering portal, a bright good sky, land of one's fathers, patrimony, inheritance, endowment, that cry for substance and structure to found one's spirit and protect one's life, that cry for a fathering God can never be fully satisfied because father brings murder near. *"Eloi, eloi lema sabachthani"* (Mark 15: 34) is indeed the archetypal cry of sonship witnessing the truth of the murderous father.

The killing father, whether repressed, enacted, or sublimated, permeates the psychoanalytic movement, obsessing Freud too in regard to his pupils and to the second sense, the next generation, brought by the sons to analytic theories. The murderous aspect continues on in each analysis, even if euphemistically named negative transference and counter-transference, or resistance, aggression, hostility, or rage. And, it appears among the schools of analysis as violent revisionism and bitter orthodoxy. Scapegoats, expulsions, pinioned feet, sterility, narrowness at intersections, and oracular readings which curse the other by discovering what is truly wrong with the other—all this keeps the configuration of Laius very present in our field. Psychoanalysis walks in its own shadow and perpetuates the shadow of its tragic myth.

JAMES HILLMAN

6. *Myth and Method*

Our route has passed dangerously close to the
Sphinx. Was Freud wrong about Oedipus or right—
as if like a hero we had to choose? We are still in
Sphinxian territory, though I think we now can see
why the riddle appears. We have been misled by the
intentional fallacy, misled into reading Freud according to his intentions. That is, Freud intended
to establish that the core complex of every analytic
drama is Oedipal. The basic content of the con-
flicted soul lies in childhood and its passions in regard to parents. Self-knowledge consists in uncover-
ing this truth.

So, we have been misled in following Freud's belief
that the *contents* of the myth are the essentials of
analysis. We have been driven either to accept that
we, like Little Hans, are really Oedipus, thus prov-
ing that this Oedipal core is universal, or to reject
this core content, thereby seeming to be free of
Freud and Freudianism.

It is not, however, the contents of the myth that
keep analysis Freudian. It is the method. Analysis
is Oedipal in *method*: inquiry as interrogation, consciousness as seeing, dialogue to find out, self-discovery by recall of early life, oracular reading of
dreams. The methods of an analysis are the *methods*

of this myth. Here we connect again with the Eranos theme of this year: Crossroads.

The Greek word for road is *hodos*, from which our "method," *meta-hodos*. Can we imagine a way beyond the narrow and killing road by Cithaeron, a way that would leave behind the dilemmas of this drama not only in content but in procedure, a way of analysis that remains a therapy, but not Oedipal, not Apollonic?

Some years ago, at Eranos, I tried to find another road. I turned to Dionysos, and to Hades, suggesting a post-Apollonic consciousness.[32] I had earlier also suggested Psyche and Eros as the myth of analysis.[33] But to my ignorance, I remained Oedipal. I was still blind to the overriding importance of method, that the deepest myth of any analysis lies in its methods.

And so Jung too does not offer a way out. The 1912 passage which opens *Wandlungen und Symbole* (and which I quoted earlier) pays tribute to Freud and Oedipus in order to leave Freud and Oedipus. In order to leave Freud and Oedipus, Jung introduced many new methods: amplification rather than association, synthetic and prospective understanding, typological relativity, the chair rather than the couch, one or two hours rather than five, participation of the analyst rather than an impartial screen. Nevertheless, the myth of Oedipus remains in the *meta-hodos* of Jungian analysis: becoming conscious

through insight, a journey to self-knowledge, a dialogue with wiser Teiresian figures, consciousness as
self-awareness, dream as oracle.

Maybe I need to demonstrate more fully what I
mean by the myth in the method and why analysis
remains Oedipal because of its methods in actual
practice. To do this, let us turn once more to Freud,
Freud as practicing analyst talking with a patient.
The patient is again Little Hans. One of Freud's
pupils then was the father of the boy. (The mother
too had been analyzed by Freud.) The father recorded the little boy's fantasies, anxieties, behaviors,
and remarks, and also what he, the father, also the
mother, replied. A long diary, verbatim, over many
months. Freud consulted regularly with the father,
seeing the actual boy only once. Freud analyzed this
case, foundational for the field of child analysis, at
one remove. His clarity about the child psyche comes
from an Apollonic distance.

We now listen in on Freud's record of that one
conversation when Freud saw and spoke with the
boy. Father and Hans together come to the Doctor.
(I shall abbreviate here and there.)

> That afternoon the father and son visited me.
> . . . The consultation was a short one. His fa-
> ther opened it by remarking that in spite of
> all the pieces of enlightenment we had given
> Hans, his fear of horses had not yet dimin-

ished. . . . As I saw the two of them sitting in front of me and at the same time heard Hans's description of his anxiety-horses, a further piece of the solution shot through my mind. . . . I asked Hans jokingly whether his horses wore eyeglasses [Freud refers to the blinders of which Hans was particularly afraid] to which he [Hans] replied that they did not. I then asked him whether his father wore eyeglasses, to which, against all the evidence, he . . . said no. . . . I then disclosed to him that he was afraid of his father, precisely because he was so fond of his mother. . . . Long before he was in the world, I went on, I had known that a little Hans would come who would be so fond of his mother that he would be bound to feel afraid of his father because of it. . . .

Freud concludes the paragraph by recounting a little scene between father and son prior to their consultation with him; the next paragraph opens with this amazing sentence:

"Does the Professor talk to God," Hans asked his father on the way home, "as he can tell all beforehand?" I should be extraordinarily proud of this recognition out of the mouth of a child, if I had not myself provoked it by my joking boastfulness. From the date of this con-

> sultation I received almost daily reports of the alterations in the little patient's condition. It was not to be expected that he should be freed from his anxiety at a single blow by the information I gave him; but . . . from that time forward he carried out a programme which I was able to announce to his father in advance.

"Does the Professor talk to God, as he can tell all beforehand?" ("*Spricht denn der Professor mit dem lieben Gott, daß er das alles vorher wissen kann?*")[34] The case of Little Hans is not only the first analysis *of* a child; it is the first analysis *by* a child, for Hans sees through the Professor's clothes, laying Freud's case bare. Freud believes he sees into Hans, past and future: before Hans was born he loved his mother—and soon after the "information I gave him," Hans could carry out "a programme which I was able to announce to his father in advance." But Hans sees through to Freud's essential nature, Freud's Moses beneath the beard.

Where Freud sees Hans's blindness—that his father quite evidently does wear glasses, so that fear of the horse with blinders reduces to fear of the Father—Hans reads Freud's inability to see that he stands in the middle of myth, unseeing. Even the phrase "a further piece of the solution shot through my mind" ("*schoss mir ein weiteres Stück der Auflösung durch den Sinn*") comes suddenly during the exchange about eyesight and blinders. Was what shot through his mind an Apollonic arrow? Is this how Apollo affects analysis: sudden insights, resolving clarities, blinding revelations? Where Freud sees the Oedipal contents in Hans, Hans sees the Oedipal method in Freud. Freud the oracle: the Professor talks with God and knows "beforehand," like Teiresias, like the oracles to which Oedipus, Laius, and Creon turn in order 'to carry out a programme.'

In the very moment of insight into Hans, Freud is blind to the process of insight itself because he is seized by its content. This is precisely how insight blinds. We are so fascinated by what we see, we do not see our seeing: the objective content of the insight stands forth and we lose the subjective factor that makes this content visible in the first place. This is the Oedipal moment in the analytical method — when surety seizes, epiphanic, following upon a long coil of unraveling and piecing together. Freud sees Oedipus in Hans because Freud's method is Oedipal. As he said: "The action of the play consists simply in the disclosure, approached step by step and artistically delayed (and comparable to the work of a psychoanalysis). . . ."[35] What Freud sees is the objectification of the myth he has imported into analysis by means of his method, that art of detection toward clarified solutions. Freud is Oedipal, our field of psychology is Oedipal because, according to Teiresias, the dominant characteristic of this blind man Oedipus lies in how his mind works, his superior *heuriskein* (440): discovering, finding, or figuring out. Precisely this analytic activity of figuring out keeps us Oedipal. We must pursue further this theme of psychoanalytic blinding.

7. *Psychoanalytic Blindness*

Blindness is the prerequisite of the Oedipal method in depth psychology, for it initiates self-searching. We start in the dark, unable to see what to do, which way to go, as if at a crossroads. We ask for light on the problems and insight into our natures. We want to see clearly what is wrong and rid our states of soul of their barrenness and blight, and thus find truly what we are. We turn to dreams as gnomic guides and piece out the puzzle step by step. Yes, to be in analysis we must be blind. That blindness is today called unconscious.

There are ways of being blind: as Oedipus whose eyes are open and cannot see, as Teiresias whose eyes are closed and is a seer. Still, both are blind. The language of light and sight and eyes permeates the play. Oedipus's self-blinding at the end of the *Tyrannos* is commonly understood as the revelation of his true character. He is concretely blind at the end because he is psychically blind at the beginning. Oedipus's blinding at the end, however, is the outcome of his method of proceeding—pursuit, questioning, getting to the truth of himself, self-discovery. Know Thyself, here, equals blindness: when, by pursuing the Oedipal method, finally I know who I am, the result is blinding, and blindness.

What Teiresias calls the "double-striking curse from father and mother both, shall drive you forth . . . with darkness in your eyes" (Grene, 416–17) results from the Oedipal attempt to see by interrogation and interpretation. Content results from method. The what that is discovered is utterly tied to the way it is discovered. The parental curses unfolded in an analysis follow from the tale into which we are enfolded by entering the original blindness that is the analytical premise: its fantasy of a journey, a *hodos*, from unconsciousness toward self-discovery via enlightenment.

For there to be an analysis at all, we must find ourselves tied to the parental world as unconsciousness, incestuously (Freud), uroborically (Jung), desiring heroically to free ourselves through insight. "I will hear nothing but of finding out the whole thing clearly" (Grene/Cook, 1065), declares Oedipus, while Jocasta's final response pleads for unconsciousness: "O Oedipus, God help you! May you never know who you are!" (Grene/Cook, 1068). Finding out who you are overcomes incestuous unconsciousness, and the analyst guides by having wider, deep-set eyes, Teiresian eyes. Analysis aims to open those of the patient by placing concrete life in the vessel (temenos, process, transference, etc.), putting out the eyes of the physical view so as to see life more clearly as a field of ignorant projections, as shadows on the wall of the cave.

The outcome is tragedy, since the "I"'s heroic effort to see is the symptom itself trying to see, and a symptom cannot see itself. That is why it is a symptom. The tragedy of Greece becomes the tragedy of psychoanalysis. As Freud said: "Every member of the audience was once a budding Oedipus in phantasy and this . . . causes everyone to recoil in horror."[36] The tragic realization that the very instrument I call my consciousness, and which I am using right now to analyze the tragedy of Oedipus, is itself Oedipal makes me recoil, not because of my fantasies, but because the horror is my own consciousness.

So analysis cannot help but confirm with case after case as empirical evidence the terrible impact of the desires, fears, hatreds, and abuses of childhood. And analysis cannot help but propound every few years new theories regarding the cursing causality of the parental imagos and the formative dynamics of early childhood. Every new theory from Freud's immediate disciples, through Klein, Kohut, and Lacan, including modern Jungianism's fascination with developmental psychology, the mother and father archetypes, sandplay and child analysis, turns to the same Oedipal ground. The empirical findings and the revelatory theories confirm the myth on which analysis, as Freud said, bases itself. Because we proceed like Oedipus, we think like Oedipus, and we find what he found.[37]

Were we to imagine therapy differently—say, as

a work in love with the mythologem of Eros and Psyche paramount; or as a work in generativity and marriage with the myths of Zeus and Hera and their struggles and their progeny; or as a work in imaginative flying and crafting with Icarus and Daedalus; or of Ares and the world of combat, anger, and destruction; or as a world of mimesis where art becomes life through desire with Pygmalion; or a work in which Hermes or Aphrodite or Persephone or Dionysos plays the principal—therapy's methods would display an altogether different nature. Would we still be assessing a human soul in terms of its origins, and would origins be equivalent to parents and childhood? Would we still be trying to 'find ourselves,' our true story, our identity? Would we still be solving riddles, reading predictions out of our dreams, treating our fantasies as oracles to tell us who we really are? Were the methods derived from other myths, analysts would less be fathers and mothers, seers and prophets. Incest and child abuse would not be prime theoretical concepts and experiential anchors. And blindness would be relocated from the definition of unconsciousness to the very act of analyzing that unconsciousness. Like Oedipus, our blindness appears in the methods we employ to see.

While Oedipus is wholly engaged in the pursuit of himself, different methods would free us from subjectivism. Our sufferings and pathologies would be less about ourselves. Instead, they might refer to the inherent difficulties of flying and crafting, say; to the art of skillful loving; to the heart-work of marriage; to the isolation of research; the pain of fighting; or to living right with Gaia's earth. The weariness, the fever, and the fret that harassed the task of writing this paper would be attributed to the paper—the *daimones* of writing, of public speaking, of Eranos, of Oedipus—not to the 'me' and 'my problem.' Unless we let go of subjectivism, how will the soul ever return to the world, to things as they are so that they receive the attention they need from us? There are other pursuits, other urgencies than those of Self. What is it to make beauty? To serve my city? Be a friend, die with dignity, love the world, remember the Gods?

I named a few themes and a few mythical personages at random. Countless tales move through the forest. The soul's meadows are carpeted with interlacing fictions. Sophocles himself, says E. R. Dodds, "held various priesthoods."[38] And the Chorus in *Oedipus* invokes many other Gods in contrast to the monomythic hero who maintains a self-righteous devotion to one God only. The Chorus asks: "O doer of dread deeds. . . . What daimon drove you on?" Oedipus replies: "Apollo it was, Apollo, friends,/ Who brought these ills" (Cook/Storr, 1318–321).

The play itself adumbrates another way of coming to the truth of one's nature. The origin of Oedi-

pus is told by a drunk in a tavern, making super-
fluous the entire procedure of oracles, prophets,
oaths, and inquisitions. Gossip, drunkenness, and
the ordinary fellowship of *demos* reveal character and
fate without the Oedipal method of self-searching
inquiry. Others tell you who you are. The play follows
this Dionysian track, for it stages in public for all
to see the agonizing intimacies of soul.

The constraints of our Oedipal fiction, nevertheless, prevent me from exploring these possibilities.
As long as I am doing a psychoanalysis of psychoanalysis, my thought is limited by the Oedipal
method: insight, clarification, discovery of what is
wrong, tracing back to parents and childhood—
Apollo, Sophocles, early Freud, Little Hans. I cannot chart the routes for other therapies—of craft
and skill, of service, of expression, of camaraderie,
of worship, of the discipline of beauty, whatever
—because the Oedipal method has defined even the
meta-hodos: becoming conscious as finding self.
Whatever myths may operate in the psyche, whatever contents we might disclose, as long as our
method remains *search for self,* these other tales will
yield only Oedipal results because we turn to them
with the same old intention. We are still seeking a
subjective identity by understanding ourselves, locating this understanding and this identity in a nar-
rative of personal development. We can't get out of
this play, this tragedy.

Pop-polytheisms and astro-mytho-typologies delude us by offering fresh new contents for identifying ourselves. The new contents are nonetheless constrained by the old method of self-discovery. We turn to a Goddess not for her sake, her *therapeia*, but for our self-realization. The transpersonal ideals of new-age psychologies defend against Apollonic anxieties with Apollonic idealizations. These serve as counter-phobic denials of the tragedy inherent in their search for self. Hence, the desperate desire to leave the Greek world altogether for Native American healing rites, Eskimo shamanism, Balinese movement, Zendo sitting, African drumming, Hindu breathing, Tantric sex. Therapy wants to leave Greece to escape Oedipus.

How much this myth is ours, how thoroughly it characterizes our psychological age, shows in the accounts we give of our miseries. What other culture—Egyptian, Hindu, Roman, tribal, traditionally Catholic, let alone that of Greece—would attribute to actual parents and actual childhoods the reason that one goes insane, is depressed, falls ill with psychic complaints, or falls out of society? And what other culture would seek the cure to those ills— not in Gods, ancestors, or cosmic forces, not in rituals, curses, demons, names, places, foods, airs, waters, that is, actual things visible and invisible— but in calling up your personal childhood and parentage from long ago and far away. What an irony that the psychology of our culture is fixated in the idea of development, thereby preventing psychology, and our culture, from the very development espoused by its idea.

Psychoanalysis offers consciousness. (I use "psychoanalysis" for the entire psychotherapeutic movement regardless of school.) Consciousness is the salvational term. Consciousness may protect, or at least give *providentia*, in regard to disaster, disease, destiny—especially the destiny of Oedipus. If we have psychological consciousness, we will not be blind. That is the assumption. The practitioners of the cult of consciousness perform its rituals at appointed hours, appointed places. In this practice, the Oedipal contents of history as determinants of fate are attested, witnessed, and confirmed by priest and penitent in emotionally gripping communion. Claiming that the practice of the cult may open the eyes through its method of subjective examination, psychoanalysis maintains a blinding to its myth that requires blindness as its premise, even defining its own blinding as insight. Furthermore, by exclusively defining consciousness as the product of its method, psychoanalysis preempts the method of becoming conscious. Its hubris is Oedipal: self-awareness is the only definition of consciousness. There is only one way: the method of subjective investigation. Outside the church, no salvation. (*Extra ecclesiam, nulla salus est!*)

Yet analysis itself is only one way, a way that offers a disciplined contribution to the skills of psychological reflection, imagination, and conversation. No small skills these, but they hardly encompass consciousness. The fisherman with his net, the soul-singer's voice with the blues, the attorney's awareness in argument, the kindergarten teacher and the nurse moving among their charges, the gardener's sense of sun, shade, soil, and moisture—these exquisitely attentive consciousnesses require no examination of subjective history. Yet, analysis would say for them to be conscious they must enter the church, go into therapy. I would rather say *the unexamined life is indeed worth living.* More: life is not a riddle; how monstrous to consider it so! "O taste and see!"[39]

8. Analysis at Colonus

I seem to have doomed psychoanalysis by maintaining its tie to Oedipus from whose tragedy, according to the tragedy, there is no escape. We have learned that substituting another myth or any number of myths will only lead back to Oedipus because of the analytical method. Fortunately, this very same myth offers a way forward. Freud stops in Thebes, with the *Tyrannos*. Sophocles dreams the myth along, as Jung advised us all to do. Let us move then from Freud to Jung by going with Oedipus to Colonus, that second Oedipus, written by Sophocles in his nineties, soon before his death in this same city, Colonus.

There can be, however, no way forward until psychoanalysis takes into itself, as thoroughly and completely as does Oedipus, the reality of its own blind inflation: that inflated insistence that it is the doctor of the sick city, of the barrenness and blight lying all around its carefully framed consulting rooms. Our location of psyche in psychology and thus our imprisoning control of it, our self-centered view of consciousness depriving the world of its mind, our reduction of the unfathomable *hodos* of the soul to the little tracks of childhood, hearing the Gods only in oracles, and that presumption that were we to set an individual consciousness straight then the city will be well again—this is delusion and this is hubris. Like Oedipus, we move to Colonus only when we recognize the blinding eye-opening truth that we are the culpable and not the cure.

The first description of Colonus comes from Antigone:

> As for this place, it is clearly a holy one
> Shady with vines and olive trees and laurel.
> The nightingales
> Make sweet music.
> (Fitzgerald, 16–19)

The Chorus says further of the holy place:

> In the glade where the grass is still
> Where the honeyed libations drip
> In the rill from the brimming spring.
> (Ibid., 157–59)

And in the famous choral poem describing Colonus, the nature of Cithaeron is utterly transformed:

> . . . leaves and berries strong
> and wine-dark ivy climbs the bough
> the sweet, sojourning nightingale
> murmurs all day long.
> . . . ever through the shadow goes

147

Dionysos reveler.
Immortal maenads in his train.

(Ibid., 672–80)

The verses go on telling of clusters of narcissus, crocus, olive trees and gray-eyed Athene, of the Muses and Aphrodite. There is much about taming horses. Bird song, the sound of waters, the limpid poems themselves show a shift from seeing to hearing. The opening line of the play is a question, the key question to resolving the Oedipal complex. Oedipus asks Antigone: "My daughter . . . where I wonder have we come to now?" In the next eighty-one lines of the play, Oedipus asks nineteen questions. These differ from the questions he asked in Thebes or were asked him by the Sphinx or asked of the oracle. He is no longer the furious inquisitor, twisting the shepherd's arm to get the full story (*Oed. Rex*, 1152).

He asks about the place, the nature and behavior of where he is now and how to adapt to it. "Hide me in the wood, so I may hear/What they are saying" (114), he says to Antigone. The Chorus says to him in the first speech, "Wanderer can you hear?" Antigone advises him: "We should give in now, and listen to them" (Fitzgerald, 171). "Sounds are the things I see" (Fitzgerald, 139). To be alive is to hear: the Chorus describes death as "without music, without dance" (1222). He learns the prayer from the Chorus by listening (*akousai*) (486). Where he could not see through in the *Tyrannos*, in the *Colonus* he can hear (*akoueté*) through Creon's deception (881). At the close, before he walks away to die, he hears his daughters wailing, hears the signal thunder and the call from the other world: "Oedipus, Oedipus! Why are you waiting? You delay too long. . . . (1627–628).

The reliance on oracles fades. He even refers to Apollo's oracle as ugly (*kaka*, 87). In anima country, the spiritual mode is passing. When one is in touch, who needs farsighted wisdoms? "There is no felicity in speaking of hidden things," says old Oedipus (Fitzgerald, 624–25). Fewer signs, seers, and prophecies: more listening close at hand. "Touch me," he says to Ismene (327), and to Antigone, ". . . let me touch you/whom I had never thought to touch again!" (Fitzgerald, 1104).

Oedipus at Colonus suffers physically as did his people in Thebes. He has fallen out of his wits into the world of touch by striking out his eyes with Jocasta's pin. This opens his eyes by shutting them from light, from seeing clearly, and from knowing as seeing. Now he knows differently. He has descended[40] from the spiritual blinding of his hubris as savior, through the psychological blinding of obsession with family, into the underside of his God, blood-crime, and catharsis: Phoebus Apollo, now wolf and raven.[41] Only in this final fall is Oedipus re-visioned by re-visioning himself.

Aristotle, in the *Poetics* (XIV) when speaking of fear and pity and the *Oedipus*, says that "the mythos ought to be constructed that, even without the eye, he who hears the tale told will thrill with horror and melt to pity." Not the eye but the ear: *katharsis* depends not on what we see, but how we hear. Aristotle in this passage—despite the basically Apollonic meaning of *katharsis* as rational clarification[42]—has placed himself within the cathartic shift from *Tyrannos* to *Colonus*.

The move from Thebes to Colonus moves the mind from seeing to hearing, moves questioning from what happened to *where are we now*, moves family from parents to children and moves children (*tekna* as he called the Thebans and now calls his daughters) from duty to love, moves the revelation of character from inquiry into origins to preparation for ends, moves saving the city by action to blessing the city by death, and moves piety from oracles to libations. These moves have brought Oedipus into anima country; Colonus is described as *argeta*: silvery, radiant, white (670).[43] This is the new land, a foreign land for a hero.

So these moves suggest another one: from Freud to Jung, a move within the myth of analysis which is our main reason for revisiting Oedipus. In the *Colonus* anima and images are more the method—the hollow pear tree where Oedipus sits down and undoes his filthy garments (1595-596). Antigone in the wild forest, without shoes, beaten by the rains (350), Ismene smiling, wearing a wide sun-hat as she returns on a Sicilian pony (313-19), the simile for Oedipus's suffering like a wild wintery wrack of waves breaking over him, coming on forever (1242-244). Anima takes the lead in the person of Antigone who provides the *hodos* (113). He calls Ismene and Antigone "my children . . . and sisters" (329). Incest shifts from literalism and taboo to sister-daughter, an accompanying double sense that guides his way. Gods are invoked of whom we heard little before— Hermes, Persephone, green Demeter. Ares who brought anger on Oedipus and fiery plague on Thebes and bright-burning Phoebus, too, fade their force. The blindness of Oedipus and of Teiresias are supplemented by the blindness of the unquiet soul. "My eyes are blind with tears/From crying for you, father," says Antigone (Fitzgerald, 1709). "To wipe them clear of sadness is impossible" (Moebius, 1711). This land flows with waters. It belongs to Poseidon. Rather than detection of wrong and correction of it, submission—to his terrible life, to death, the Gods, and to Theseus, the younger king.

The bond between Theseus and Oedipus repeats,

and redeems, the homoerotic love so disastrous for Laius. Although the ancestral ("before his birth") curse of Thebes continues in Oedipus's cursing of his own sons who have driven him out, he gives his blessing to another man's son, Theseus. The feeling between them is conferred not by forceful passion in the style of Laius, but by submission. Oedipus transmits the power of blessing by surrender to his weakness. He says to Theseus, "I come to give you something, and the gift/Is my own beaten self [*athlion demas*]" (Fitzgerald, 576). Does this indicate how the old fathering analyst advances the homoerotic transference between junior and senior men? The relationship advances to a blessing, not because the elder confers status, wisdom, or protection, but by his beseeching refuge for his beaten self in the younger's territory. He says, "For Oedipus is not the strength he was" (110). Yet, he says, "When I am nothing, my worth begins" (393).[44] Surrender as blessing.

Freud, too, says this is the way of passing the Oedipal complex: submission to the other without fear of castration. (Though the man to whom one submits, Sophocles might add, must be of virtue, for Oedipus submits neither to Creon nor Polyneices.) That passing, that dissolution, of the Oedipus complex— Freud's term is *"Untergang"*—occurs graphically in the *Colonus*. Oedipus leaves by way of a steep downward path (*katarrakten hodon*). Whether as submission, or as a second undersense (*hyponoia*), or as underworld, the way down of Oedipus is the way up of the psyche. The messenger describes his going:

> Some gentle, painless cleaving of earth's base;
> For without wailing or disease or pain
> He passed away—an end most marvellous.
> (Storr, 1660–663)

In this play analysis itself seems surpassed, for contentment yields understanding, rather than understanding, contentment. Finding out is not the way, does not yield meaning, nor does it save from tragedy. For as Oedipus says and as Freud repeats, the tragedy was all known long ago, before birth (970). The focus is no longer "remember what happened." Instead, Oedipus says in his final line, "remember me" (1553), himself passing away into *memoria*, into the marvelous, conscious of becoming myth. Neither knowing, nor truth, nor meaning matters so much in anima country. Instead, hearing, beauty, nature, blessing, loyalty, service, dying, and love. He says to Antigone:

> Press close to me, child,
> Be rooted in your father's arms; rest now
> From the cruel separation, the going and coming.
> (Fitzgerald, 1112–114)

And at the close to his daughters:

JAMES HILLMAN

Children, this day your father is gone from you.
Everything about him dies; this rigorous attention to his needs may now be dropped. I know
how hard it was. Yet it was made lighter by one
word—love [*philein*].

(Moebius, 1611–617)

9. The Changeless and the Changing
Ethos and Daimon

Many changes between *Tyrannos* and *Colonus*, but not the character of the main character.[45] Oedipus is still a savior-hero, before of Thebes, now of Colonus by protecting it with his tomb. He still asks questions, wants to know; still relies on wits, in dealing with Creon and Polyneices; still sent by Apollo (665), declaring himself a sober, wineless man (*nephon aoinos*) (100) who expects Apollo's word to be fulfilled (102). He still fights, heroically grappling Creon. The family pull remains; Creon and Polyneices remind him of mother and father, murder and Thebes. They want his daughters and his death to be located in the old place. He is still concerned with *polis*, saying to Theseus in a last blessing: "I pray that you and this your land and all your people may be blessed" (Fitzgerald, 1553), still uniting king, land, and people in one. The trait of secrecy in his character, from his origins in hiddenness and as paranoid counterpart to his public identity, also persists. For he commands Theseus in that same speech to come to the grave "Alone. Alone because I cannot disclose it/to any of your men or to my children/Much as I love them. . . ./ Keep it secret always. . ." (Fitzgerald, 1528–530). A consistency of *ethos* or character remains (*Poetics* XV).

The distinction between what changes and what does not change is crucial to psychotherapy. To work on the changeless as if it could be changed or to miss the changes by fixing upon intractable complexes—these are indeed unhappy therapeutic errors. The *ergon* of analysis changes us and does not change us. The same and the different are indeed basic categories. They are not merely perspectives, as if with one eye we can see all the differences psychoanalysis makes, while with the other eye everything seems to have stayed the same. Oedipus provides a background for this crucial distinction between what does and what does not change. The tenor, the landscape, the images, the method all change. Preparing for death, he has been moved into anima country. The sister-daughter "who served my naked eyepits as their eyes" (Fitzgerald, 867) has given him a different vision.

Analysis can learn from this that its work is less to change character than to release soul from the tyranny of character, to distinguish between *ethos* and *daimon*, and so to serve *daimon*, a *therapeia* of *daimon*. As Henry Corbin said: not your individuation is the aim of the work but the individuation of the angel. Hence, at the end, Oedipus vanishes and the daughters remain visible—Jung's *esse in anima*, being in soul (*CW* 6, §77), displayed as dramatic reality.

The process of analytical work is artistically delayed, as Freud said, though not, as he said, to unravel and disclose. Step by step, the vision of the *daimon* leads the blindness of character, as Antigone leads Oedipus, into a foreign land, the white city, *la terre pure*. "He died as he had wished, in a foreign land," says Antigone (1708). Of course, his questions are all about this foreign land rather than about himself, for the habitual *ethos* of self-study, the psychodynamics of Oedipus, offers nothing about where he is now. The land has changed because the anima *daimon* has changed from killing mother mountain to benign grove of Goddesses, from Furies to Eumenides, from suicidal queen mother-wife and suicidal Sphinx, and possible nympholepsy, to loving sister-daughters. With the death of Oedipus at Colonus, psychoanalysis based in this myth passes from *ethos* to *daimon*, from psychodynamics to psychodaimonics. Character and soul go their separate ways. Apollonic kingship and its blindness, family history cursed with literalism and prophecy, the method of inquiry for problem solving—all leave this earthly scene. The daughter-sister and the city go on.

If the eternality of Oedipus as a hero, as a drama, and as a timeless myth of the psyche is assured at the close of the *Colonus* by traditional signs of immortality—lightning, vanishing, opening to the other world[46]—the *actual immortality is presented as continuity,* as attachment to the *agon* of life. Antigone goes back to Thebes. That's what actually goes on: the soul and the city. In her last speech at the very end of the *Colonus* she says: "Return us to the other world of Thebes," which she calls *Ogygious* (1770),[47] locating the mythical, primal, imaginal place in the actual city of Thebes, that cursed pathologized place. *For the soul, the other world is in this world, visible, continuing, and here.*

10. Postscript

I ask to conclude with a postscript about the act of speaking, to give an account of my reasoning in accepting to speak of psychoanalysis at Eranos yet again. How much does one have to say, after all? Do we not revolve around the same themes, strike the same chords, even if in different keys and rhythms. But I did not come for the reason of newness, because of something new to say. This theme of Apollonic blindness was addressed here often in earlier papers. Moreover, Freud and Jung have been the pivotal figures for my twistings and turnings year after year. And certainly I do not come to help maintain a tradition, that is, for reasons of oldness. A tradition lives in the silent devotion of attendance: it does not require speaking. Time, neither as newness nor oldness, provides justification.

At first I accepted out of loyalty and affection and a need for the nourishment given by this picnic, this *eranos*. I have since recognized that the presentation of this paper is a presentation of self, of Oedipal self, of a blind man in a sick city, struggling with the Apollonic curse of his world, psychoanalysis. The play brought words of self-revelation; I did not realize at first that I was in the play, that the drama was so powerful, Freud so keen-scented, and that this play plays through the inquiring mind and heuristic method of our culture from which I have not escaped. I did not recognize that it was I who could not hear to the heart of my own discourse. Even my asking and answering "Why did I come, why do I speak?" is Oedipal. Only when Oedipus goes under the hill, only as he walks away from us, might the nightingales, the freshening waters of Poseidon, and the greening of Demeter touch our field, a psychology of anima released from the tyranny of Oedipus. "Oedipus, Oedipus! Why are you waiting? You delay too long to go!" (Fitzgerald, 1627–628).

1. Sigmund Freud, *The Interpretation of Dreams*, trans. A. A. Brill, Modern Library (New York: Random House, 1938); and *The Interpretation of Dreams*, trans. James Strachey (London: Allen & Unwin, 1954).

2. Sigmund Freud, *The Origins of Psychoanalysis: Letters to Wilhelm Fliess* (London: Imago, 1954), letter dated 15 October 1897.

3. Cited from an interview with C. G. Jung, *Good Housekeeping*, December 1961, as quoted in Edward Edinger, *Ego and Archetype* (Harmondsworth: Penguin), 101.

4. Sigmund Freud, "Analysis of a Phobia in a Five-Year-Old Boy," in *Collected Papers* 3:253. "*Er ist wirklich ein kleiner Oedipus . . .*," *Jahrbuch für psychoanalytische und psychopathologische Forschungen* 1/1 (1909): 84.

5. "All this did not happen at one time but always is so . . .," Sallustius, *Concerning the Gods and the Universe*, ed. and trans. A. D. Nock (Hildesheim: Ulms, 1966), §IV.

6. The Sophocles texts of *Oedipus Tyrannos* and *Oedipus Epi Kolonus* referred to are those published in the Loeb Classical Library, *Sophocles*, vol. 1 (Cambridge: Harvard University Press and London: Heinemann [1912], 1981). Translations into English quoted are those of Albert Cook, in A. Cook and Edwin Dolin, eds., *An Anthology of Greek Tragedy* (Dallas: Spring Publications [1972], 1981); F. Storr, *Sophocles*, vol. 1; E. F. Watling (Harmondsworth: Penguin, 1947); Robert Fagles (Harmondsworth: Penguin, 1982); David Grene (*Oed. Tyr.*) and Robert Fitzgerald (*Oed. Kol.*) in *Sophocles I* (Chicago: University of Chicago Press,

1954); Sir George Young (London: Dent [1906], 1947);
William Moebius (*Oed. Kol.*) in *Greek Tragedy*. Also consulted: A. C. Pearson, *Sophocles Fabulae*, Oxford Classical
Texts ([1924], 1961); my line enumerations attempt to
follow those of Pearson and Storr.

7. *CW* 10, pp. 179–93.

8. Seth Benardete, "Sophocles' Oedipus Tyrannus," in
Thomas Woodard, ed., *Sophocles* (Englewood Cliffs: Pren-
tice-Hall, 1966), 109.

9. Cf. Richmond Lattimore, "Sophocles: *Oedipus Tyrannus*,"
in *Oedipus, Myth and Dramatic Form*, ed. J. L. Sanderson
and E. Zimmerman (Boston: Houghton Mifflin, 1968),
295–97. The stories of Cithaeron are collected in W. H.
Roscher, *Ausführliches Lexikon der griechischen und römischen
Mythologie*, II/I, ss. 1208–209 (Hildesheim: Ulms, 1965).

10. Roscher, *Ausführliches Lexikon*, V, ss. 207–10.

11. *Pausanias's Description of Greece*, translated with a commen-
tary by J. G. Frazer, V,ix.3.9 (p. 20) (New York: Biblio and
Tannen, 1965).

12. Karl Kerényi, *The Heroes of the Greeks* (London: Thames
and Hudson, 1959), 92.

13. C. G. Jung, *CW* 5, §264: "Little did he know that the riddle of the Sphinx can never be solved merely by the wit
of man"; §265: "The riddle of the Sphinx was *herself*—
the terrible mother-imago, which Oedipus would not
take as a warning." *CW* 10, §714: "Oedipus . . . fell vic-

tim to his tragic fate, because he thought he had answered the question. It was the Sphinx itself that he ought to have answered and not its facade."

14. Kurt Koffka, *Principles of Gestalt Psychology* (London: Routledge and Kegan Paul, 1936), 407 is discussed in my *Emotion* (London: Routledge and Kegan Paul, 1960), 139–41.

15. I refer here to the *materia signata* or *materia individualis* of Thomas Aquinas.

16. Adolf Guggenbühl-Craig, "Der nur gute Vater," *Gorgo* 12 (1987): 31–42.

17. Imitation (*mimesis*) may serve as a first entry into initiation, as an exercise in behaving in advance of oneself. One copies or identifies with an idealized model (*eikon*), devoutly hoping the image will carry one into a desired state of soul. The model remains effective as long as we attend it with observances (*devotio, dulia*). Imitation, therefore, keeps us ritually tied to an icon, in its cult, and enhanced by its power. Initiation, however, begins in bewilderment and setback, a darkness characterized by loss of model and loss of power. Naked, toothless, bleeding, in pain, alone, unequal to the task and in need of elders, feeling terrifyingly young—these are the initiatory experiences. They shatter the icons of remembrance, and devotions provide no protection. These experiences, ritualized in ceremonies, recounted in fairy tales, and lived in a psychoanalysis, are behaved in the crises brought especially by the underworld divinities, or the chthonic aspect of others, Gods of love and com-

bat, of risk and disease, of childbirth and marriage, and by the angels of the biblical Lord. One endures in the midst of an event in which is the God. The only model remaining is the event and its images that govern behavior in the event. One becomes who one is, finds one's name, by having nothing other than the being one is, a being who behaves images. In Gabriel Marcel's terms, we are moved from *having* to *being* and in Jung's, "being in soul," *esse in anima.*

18. H. B. Forman, ed., *The Letters of John Keats* (London: Reeves and Turner, 1895), letter of April 1819 to his brother. I have expanded on "soul-making" in my *Re-Visioning Psychology* (New York: Harper & Row, 1975), 50f., 110f., et passim.

19. The idea of "counter-education" derives from Marsilio Ficino; cf. my *Re-Visioning Psychology*, 201, 133, 163.

20. Heraclitus, Diels-Kranz, frg. 93.

21. Benardete, "Sophocles' Oedipus Tyrannus."

22. Marie Delcourt, *Oedipe ou la légende du conquérant* (Paris: Belles Lettres, 1981), 141n.

23. Jean-Pierre Vernant, "Ambiguity and Reversal: On the Enigmatic Structure of *Oedipus Rex*," *New Literary History* 9 (1977–78) republished in Erich Segal, ed., *Greek Tragedy* (New York: Harper & Row, 1983), 191–92.

24. Vernant, "Ambiguity," 189, credits the idea to W. B. Stanford's "1939 study of ambiguity in Greek literature."

25. Paul Ricoeur, *Freud and Philosophy* (New Haven: Yale University Press, 1970), 519. That ambiguity should be the hallmark of Greek tragedy, especially its heroic single-mindedness (e.g., Oedipus, Hippolytus, Ajax, Medea, Antigone, Pentheus), belongs appropriately to the God of theater, Dionysos. His epithets and images—the "womanly man," both little child and darkbearded wild-man, God of both black and white maenadism (Dodds), of comings and goings (Otto), and of borderline situations (Kerényi), who is both a phallic force yet never a hero—express the double-tongued ambiguity of life (*zoe*), where generation and decomposition are inseparable, and of theater where every word is addressed both to the characters in the play and to the audience outside the play. Because this loosening of "unilateral meaning" (Vernant, "Ambiguity") threatens rational mentality, Dionysos, God of Ambiguity, is called the "loosener," the "undivided," and mad, since he does not separate the "both" into an either/or. See further on Dionysian epithets and images in my *The Myth of Analysis* (Evanston: Northwestern University Press, 1972), 258–85.

26. The union of king-and-king's son—as for instance depicted in "The Book of Lambspring," in *The Hermetic Museum* (London: Watkins [1893], 1953), 1: 296–305—shows the importance of the senex-et-puer motif in alchemy. Cf. my "Senex and Puer," *Eranos Jahrbuch 36—1967.*

27. On Laius and the invention of pederasty, see K. J. Dover, *Greek Homosexuality* (New York: Vintage Books, 1980), 198–200.

28. Paul Friedländer, *Plato*, 3 vols., Bollingen Series (New York: Pantheon, 1964), 2: 38.

29. Robert Stein, *Incest and Human Love* (Dallas: Spring Publications [1973], 1984), chap. 7 on Oedipus.

30. Eva Keuls, *The Reign of the Phallus* (New York: Harper & Row, 1985), 299.

31. Stein, *Incest and Human Love*, chap. 4, "The Incest Wound."

32. Cf. "First Adam, Then Eve," *Eranos Jahrbuch 38—1969*; "The Dream and the Underworld," *Eranos Jahrbuch 41—1972*.

33. Cf. "On Psychological Creativity," *Eranos Jahrbuch 35—1966*.

34. "Analysis of a Phobia in a Five-Year-Old Boy": I thank Dr. Joseph Cambray for calling my attention to Hans's remark. *Jahrbuch f. psychoanalytische*, 29.

35. Ibid.

36. Sigmund Freud, *Origins of Psychoanalysis*.

37. The core of blindness is belief. Seeing is believing. What we clearly see convinces us that we see clearly. The core belief of analysis states that personal disorder develops within family. The myth of family fuses with the method of analysis as the reconstruction of personal development. When "I summon up remembrance of things past" (W. Shakespeare, *Sonnet 30*), my analysis is secular and bourgeois, because those things, that past, are bound in the myth of family and of a particularly European variety. That family may exist still in white middle-class districts

that provide the population for the Oedipal cult of therapy, but that family is hardly present in the city at large. That city of black, brown, beige, olive, yellow—and tinged all through its soul with blues—seeks its cure less in self-searching sessions of sweet silent thought than in the streets.

"Secular" and "bourgeois" are other words for the fallen soul exiled in facticity. As long as the soul is in exile, as Corbin said at Eranos so often and so fervently, we see things only with the eyes of the exiled, remember the past only in its facticity, and imagine the way out only as progressive development. (Cf. Henry Corbin, "L'Imago Templi face aux normes profanes," *Eranos Jahrbuch 43—1974*, 183–254, partially in English in *Spring 1975* and fully in English in *Temple and Contemplation* [London and New York: KPI Islamic Publications, 1986].) But there is no development out of exile, since exile does not progress and the notion of development itself is the secular expression for the hope to return, for restoration. So, the therapeutic task is not reconstruction of the past and the family, but reconstruction of the Temple which restores the city to remembrance of its soul. Consequently, the urge to go into therapy in order to get out of family presents the soul's desire to return from facticity in which it feels daily exile.

38. E. R. Dodds, "On Misunderstanding the *Oedipus Rex*," *Greece and Rome* 13 (1966): part iii.

39. Psalm 34:8.

40. Cf. James Schroeter, "The Four Fathers: Symbolism in *Oedipus Rex*," in Albert Cook, ed., *Oedipus Rex: A Mirror*

for Greek Drama (Prospect Heights, Ill.: Waveland Press [1963], 1982), 131–33.

41. Cf. Karl Kerényi, *Apollo* (Dallas: Spring Publications, 1983), 56.

42. Cf. Martha C. Nussbaum, "Luck and the Tragic Emotions," in her *The Fragility of Goodness* (Cambridge: Cambridge University Press, 1986), where she claims that the history of the term *katharsis* shows its "primary, ongoing, central meaning is roughly one of 'clearing up' or 'clarification.' "

43. Cf. my "Silver and the White Earth," *Spring 1980*: 21–48 and *Spring 1981*: 21–66 on the alchemical and psychological significance of silver as color of anima.

44. Some translations of line 393 are "Am I made man in the hour when I cease to be?" (Watling); "When I am finished, I suppose I am strong!" (Fitzgerald); "So, when I cease to be, my worth begins" (Storr); "When I am nothing, then am I a man?" (Whitman). Refer to note 6 for complete references.

45. "It has long since been recognized that Oedipus, in fundamental character, is still the same as ever. . . . Not only his character but his external fate remains unchanged." Cedric H. Whitman, "Apocalypse: *Oedipus at Colonus*," in *Sophocles: A Study in Heroic Humanism* (Cambridge: Harvard University Press, 1951), 199.

46. Gregory Nagy, *The Best of the Achaeans* (Baltimore: Johns Hopkins University Press, 1979), 190–95 on thunderbolts

and gusts of wind, both of which are mentioned by denial in *Colonus* (1558–559), and thunderbolts directly in 1515.

47. Cf. "Ogygos" in Roscher, *Ausführliches Lexikon* III/1, 683–94. Besides being a name of the first king of Thebes, a general epithet for its founding patron (or pattern), for the city of Thebes itself, and one of its seven gates, Ogygos is a name of Dionysos, Poseidon, Okeanos, and of a Titan (689), as well as of the tempting water-world of Kalypso's isle. The word suggests the hidden deeps of the oceanic imagination, the titanic aspect of the primordial *Ur-welt*, or the Imaginal as *"das Unermessliche und Ungeheure"* (693).

MYTHOLOGY BY KARL KERÉNYI

Hermes: Guide of Souls

Karl Kerényi, mythographer, classicist, and friend of Jung, here presents a beautiful, authoritative study of the great God whom the Greeks revered as Guide of Souls. Chapters on Hermes and Night, Hermes and Eros, Hermes and the Goddesses illuminate the complex role of Hermes in classical mythology, while also providing an archetypal background for the guiding of souls in psychotherapy. Includes a preface by Magda Kerényi on the author's "special personal relation" to the God. (104 pp.)

Athene
Virgin and Mother in Greek Religion

The Awesome Goddess who affects the fates of both women and men. Athene unites the virginal father's-daughter and the encouraging mother of the spirit— illuminating equally the competent, practical housewife and the aggressive, male suited professional woman. Mythological background of communal and political consciousness, individuality, and the power of mind. With a psychological postscript by Murray Stein. Scholarly apparatus, index. (106 pp.)

Goddesses of Sun and Moon

Restoring passionate feminine consciousness to its rightful place both in politics and in the economy of the psyche, these four papers explore the mythemes of Circe, the enchantress; Medea, the murderess; Aphrodite, the golden one; and Niobe of the Moon. Together they lend a deep psychological orientation to some of our most puzzling and controversial issues: feminism, the occult, aesthetics, madness, dreams, even terrorism. (84 pp.)

Spring Publications, Inc.
299 East Quassett Road, Woodstock, CT 06281